SOLUTION PROSPECTS

"The beginnings of the revolution and the Kurdish question in Syria/Rojava" With Mazloum Abdi

Polat Jan

SOLUTION PROSPECTS

"The beginnings of the revolution and the Kurdish question in Syria/Rojava" With Mazloum Abdi

By: **Polat Jan**

Tranalated by: Miran Afrin

© **All rights reserved**. No part of this book may be reproduced in any form or by any electronic or mechanical means (including photocopying recording, or information storage and retrieval) without permission in writing from the author.

To Vînar ...

Contents

The second edition introduction 7

Who is Mazloum Abdi? 11

Introduction 15

Chapter one 21

The concept of the revolution and its practical applications

The Second Chapter 65

The revolution in Syria, and the positions of the Kurdish movement regarding it

The Third Chapter 167

The Political Project

The second edition introduction

A decade ago, in the autumn of 2011, in the midst of the heat of the Syrian protests, fierce debates erupted over the parties' positions on the protests, the relations between the parties and each party's projects, programs, alliances and tactics. The debates, rumors and media campaigns were progressing in parallel with the heat of the demonstrations, murders, arrests, the tendency to militarize the mass movement, the Islamization of demands and speech, and so on.

The general atmosphere at that time cast a shadow over the Kurdish street, which each side headed towards a different direction, as well as the approach of each side differed from the other side and from the opposition, which smelled Islamism and Brotherhood breaths.

At that time, we conducted these extensive dialogues and consultations in explaining, discussing, and responding to what is going on in the corridors of politics and in the Kurdish and Syrian street. We conducted a simplified and practical definition of the self-administration project, the third-line approach, the prospects for self-administration, the organization of the Kurdish community, and the establishment of a self-defensive system that will become in the next few years of the Syrian crisis one of the most prominent players in the country and its fame will reach the far places of the world.

At that time, we were all working and moving in complete secrecy and with fake names and working in complete silence in the process of theoretical, intellectual and practical preparation for building democratic self-administration and establishing the first secret cells for the protection units.

The pillars of Kurdish institutions were established in western Kurdistan. This book of dialogue was created in those circumstances to be a guide for all those who work in those conditions and are active among the masses. Those who are confronting the opposition and the aggressors and want to disprove their claims and excuses. It is also a book to introduce the project we are working on and trying to illuminate and organize the streets of Kurdistan.

Ten years after the revolution or the Syrian crisis, and eight years after the July 19 revolution, many changes, retreats, destructions, and lineups have taken place.

Simultaneously with international interventions, regional advances, and the savagery of Islamic groups, the number of forces that had been secret cells until a decade ago rose to tens of thousands, transforming self-government into a tangible and practical reality and transforming the situation of the Kurds. And made them an important player in Syria and the region. In recent years, the Kurds and their Arab and Syriac allies have made thousands of great sacrifices in the life of the Syrian massacre, and they have been able to maintain their unity and break the dominance of terrorism, achieve historic victories, liberate the land and the people. They were able to create a democratic model despite the fact that Efrin, Shahba, Gri spi and Sarkaniyeh were exposed to the disgusting occupation of Turkey.

After more than a decade of preparing this book of dialogue, and as part of an important historical document, which represents a sensitive and precise period of the life of the Kurdish people in western Kurdistan and the life of Syria in general, we decided to publish it again. Except for the introduction and a brief explanation about Mr. Mazlum Abdi, we will make it available to the public without change and as it was.

This book will be an opportunity to reactivate and sharpen the memory, return to the beginnings of the revolution, learn about how revolutionary Kurdish leaders thought during that period, and restore discussions and questions at the time.

And how many ideas and imaginations turned into concrete facts, and theoretical projects into effective institutions, forces, councils, and administration. Many of the facts of the day demonstrated the rightness and legitimacy of the project and the approach chosen by the leaders of the self-administration for their people despite all the shortcomings and defects experienced during the past period of obstacles; However, it is considered the most effective in the hell of Syria.

This book is part of the theoretical and intellectual legacy of the Rojava revolution and subsequently a humanitarian participation with the Kurdish brothers in other parts of Kurdistan and the rest of the peoples whose fate and causes are similar with the Kurdish people in western Kurdistan. Hoping that all peoples, especially the Kurdish people, will be liberated in all parts of Kurdistan.

Polat Jan

30-06-2020

Who is Mazloum Abdi?

Born in 1967 in the Kobani region, studied elementary class in Kobani, preparatory and secondary class in Aleppo, entered the Faculty of Architecture at the University of Aleppo, and was then a political activist student at the university, who soon left engineering seats to devote himself entirely to political and revolutionary work in all regions of western Kurdistan. He was influenced by the Kurdish revolutionary movement. He worked in many national fields such as the revolutionary media, student organization, and clandestine political work, subjected to arrest and prosecution by the Syrian security several times.

He left Syria and western Kurdistan, heading to the mountains of Kurdistan to participate in the armed revolution, where he promoted rapidly in the military leadership. He was seriously injured in a battle in 1995, after which he was forced to move to Europe to receive treatment. From there he continued his political, diplomatic and administrative work.

At the end of the year 2000, he returned to Kurdistan and continued his political struggle in many regions in southern Kurdistan and Iraq, and he trained many military and political strugglers cadres for work in Syria and western Kurdistan.

With the outbreak of demonstrations in Syria in 2011, Mazloum Abdi, accompanied by a group of these militants, moved to western Kurdistan to work secretly politically, militarily and organizationally, and he was as the primary (hidden) responsible for

All organizational, political and military matters in Syria and western Kurdistan, he was the architect of the Rojava Revolution, the founding of the People's Protection Units and the coordinator of military operations that began in Serekaniye at the end of 2012 to the present day.

When the Syrian Democratic Forces was established in the autumn of 2015, Mazloum Abdi was appointed as the commander-in-chief of these forces, in coordination with the international coalition, which had fought many successful battles and military campaigns such as the liberation of the Al-Hawl, Ash Shaddadi, Tishreen Dam,

Manbij, Tabqa, Raqqa, and Deir Ezzor, and was able to eliminate the alleged ISIS succession in Baguz March of 2019.

The name of Mazloum Abdi appeared in the media and in Kurdish and international public opinion during the Turkish attack on the cities of Serekaniye and Geri Spi.

Mazloum Abdi is known for his calm, humble, political and organizational skill, rational, understanding and practical in his political approaches, and he is one of the main theorists of the project of self-administration in western Kurdistan, as well as one of the founders of the People's Protection Units and the Syrian Democratic Forces.

Introduction

On December 17, 2010, as a protest against the injustice he got, the young Tunisian Mohamed Bouazizi set fire to his body; Soon, popular demonstrations erupted in the country, which lasted for an entire month, which prompted the Tunisian President Zine Al Abidine Ben Ali to flee outside Tunisia on January 14, 2011. These demonstrations were the first spark of the revolutions (the Arab Spring) or as we call it (the spring of peoples); A similar movement exploded in Egypt, Yemen, Libya and Bahrain, until it reached Syria on 15 of March 2011.

The main underlying cause of the wave of popular demonstrations and protests or revolutions at the time was the rampant corruption in the body of governance across the countries of the region, in addition to the injustice and the dire living conditions of the crushed classes, the torture system and prisons, the intelligence security mentality in dealing with political, social and economic problems, and the lack of Security, freedom of expression, political freedoms, as well as sectarian, tribal, ethnic, and national sensibilities ...

The flames of these revolutions reached Syria, and its situation was not better than the rest of the repressive regimes in the region. Besides of the accumulation of its internal issues and dilemmas in relation to national, ethnic problems issues, Sectarianism and regionalism.

The demonstrations started from Daraa, and quickly spread throughout the country. The Syrian regime did not hesitate to suppress the demonstrations and kill the demonstrators; So the other side hit back hard, Here, the movement directed more violence and counter-violence.

Regional, Arab and international powers did not stand idly by about what happened in Syria, so different interests overlapped and papers mixed and floated on the surface of different plans, projects and trends and their repercussions emerged inside the Syrian interior; Various frameworks formed and new lineups occurred in the country and the region.

Nine months have passed since the start of the demonstrations in Syria, without any signs of an international solution or a settlement that satisfies the uprising people or relieves the fearful parties of any success for the Islamists; Especially since the revolution soon took a religious and sectarian Islamic trend.

In the matter of the Kurdish people in Rojava (western Kurdistan), the general situation of the Kurds did not differ much from the conditions of the entire persecuted Syrian people, and on top of that there was a Kurdish national issue in Syria; The cause of a people oppressed nationally, politically, culturally, economically and nationally.

The Kurdish people in Rojava suffered badly due to the suppression by the authorities over the decades of the rule of the Ba'ath regime, so they remained devoid of Syrian nationality, their lands were confiscated, their areas were Arabized, their language and culture were prevented from circulating, and prevented them from learning their language and spread it the activists and politician were always subjected to distress by the Syrian regime; So The Kurdish people in Rojava were a forerunner to the uprising against this repressive and chauvinistic regime when there were no revolutions or demonstrations (the Arab Spring); On the 12th of March 2004 the spark of the March uprising started from the city of Qamishlo and turned into a massive uprising that swept the entire Kurdish regions in Syria from Afrin to Derek; The Kurds had their own political history at the Syrian patriotic and Kurdish national levels, and consequently many different political trends emerged in the region, and this was evident in the midst of the Syrian revolution, so the positions of the various Kurdish parties thereof, their political visions and the ways in which they participated in it became clear.

As soon as the demonstrations began in Daraa, they resonated in the Kurdish cities in the far north, from Qamishlo and Amoda, through Kobani to Afrin, youth coordination formed, the parties split, multiplied and distributed over the political frameworks of the Syrian opposition, and the various Kurdish parties adopted many projects of the various Arab-Sunni opposition, whether it is the Syrian National Council, the coordination body, or other different frameworks here and there.

In the midst of the eruptive mass movement and its continuation without achieving a decisive victory, and in the midst of the variation of the Kurdish discourse and the competition of its parties, a lot of old-new discussions appeared, and the mutual accusations flew into the Kurdish space, which created a lot of ambiguity within the Kurdish street, so the names differed and the term contradicted Between the name and the title; What is between the concepts of revolution, patriotism, the Kurdish nationalist dimension, private Kurdish projects, the overlap between Rojava (western Kurdistan) and the rest of the parts, the various Kurdish parties contradiction, youth coordination, brotherhood and Islamization of the Syrian revolution, militarization and the dangers of civil war, Turkish ambitions and projects, relations with the Syrian regime, Kurdish institutions, protection of the region, societal organization, self-administration and the possibility of its practical application ... Several different issues that occupied and still stand in the Kurdish public opinion emerged In Rojava, which was the focus of the questions I asked on Mr. Mazloum Abdi; And the answers that it contained included in this book.

Dozens of friends from journalists, politicians, and Kurdish activists contributed to preparing this work by sending their questions (thank you) to present it to Mr. Mazloum Abdi, who is one of the senior Kurdish leaders in Rojava (western Kurdistan), while he was - During that period - wandering secretly between the cities, villages and regions of Rojava without stopping to lead the process of implementing the project of self-administration, institution-building and organization of the masses, and laying sound foundations for a political process more appropriate to the specificities of our regions.

As a result of the security tension that prevailed in the region at the time, the task of conducting these extensive dialogues had to be divided over a period of time that lasted for more than a month; It started from the Sheikh Maksoud neighborhood in Aleppo and ended in one of Derek villages in the far northeast.

Our book will be the mouthpiece of everyone throughout the cities and regions of Rojava. It raises their questions, inquiries, criticisms, proposals and legitimate objections, so that they receive detailed answers in the explanation and simplification by one of the senior Kurdish leaders throughout the region; Regardless of whether everyone agrees with him or not, he answers questions from his political, intellectual and organizational convictions and background, and his future visions that may be right or wrong ...

So let us leave the judgment to the readers and the coming future.

Winter - 2011

CHAPTER ONE

The concept of the revolution and its practical applications

P.J - Let's start with an obvious question, about a word that has become on every tongue, a word its readings and definitions differ and that all bear on it whatever they like according to their backgrounds, goals and vision. Here I mean the word "revolution". You, what is your definition of the revolution?

M.A: We define the revolution within the framework of a democratic civilization, where the function of the revolution lies in removing obstacles in front of democratic civilization. We believe in the existence of a moral and political society within the human community; It is a natural accumulation of human experiences from antiquity to the present day, which has been subjected to numerous breakdowns and obstacles by authoritarian regimes throughout. When that (oppressive) power is removed, society will self-organize without need the state and its powers, and thus society will naturally evolve. Here, the job of the revolution lies in overcoming these obstacles and removing oppressive power, this is the function of the revolutionaries in the first place. The revolution (according to our understanding) does not mean that we should destroy an authority or a state in order to build in its place another authority, or another state, on the contrary; The revolution is the process of building a completely new natural social order and not merely a process of demolishing, repairing or refining the old one.

- There have been many revolutions throughout history, and hitherto, we are today live a year of revolutions; In other words, what is known as the 2011 revolutions, what is the background or reasons for such outbreaks?

The appearance of such revolutions in the Middle East is a natural thing, yet historical causes and accumulations from ancient times show the truth of the Middle East. The Middle East is an independent civilization, and we can say: The Middle East is the basic civilization in the history of humanity, and this civilization was destroyed before a thousand years, especially in the past two centuries, with the emergence of capitalism; Therefore, the peoples of the Middle East could not prove themselves. So the revolution in the Middle East is a revolution that recovers its stolen history, and proves its culture and identity. The system in the Middle East is not derived from the culture of this land, but was imposed externally by capitalist regimes, especially after the First World War. And the people in the Middle East do not accept this reality, so they are revolting against it ... This is the truth of these revolutions today. On the other hand, the nation-state was built after the Second World War, and it lasted for more than 60 years, but this dominant philosophy did not succeed, and the people revolt against this mentality, and this national project continues; That is, the nation state with difficulty, and cannot lead society, has actually lost its meaning, and defends itself as a broken machine that harms more than good. And society has become unacceptable to this, which is the main reason for these revolutions. The revolution that started from Tunisia in the character of Bouazizi had previously its objective conditions, and Bouazizi was the spark that blew up the things originally prepared for the explosion.

- These revolutions have been called by many names such as (the Arab Spring, the Middle East spring, and the spring of peoples' revolutions ... and other similar names) , so what do you name it ?

We cannot limit the revolution to one people, to one nationality, the revolution that has started includes all the peoples of the Middle East, because there are common denominators between these peoples who live under tyranny. This revolution, or rather the revolutions are revolutions of the people of the entire Middle East. Kurdistan is the center of these revolutions. Yes, and there is a reason for this. Because this is a revolutionary stage, and the Kurdish people are the most in need of the revolution, and it must be the biggest beneficiary at this stage, there is no revolution in the Middle East without the Kurds, I mean the Kurdish people in the four parts, and not only linked to the Arabs. The Kurdish people will participate in the revolution as one people. It is true that the 2011 revolution started in Tunisia, but we started a revolutionary period as Kurds since 2006, especially in northern Kurdistan.

And that was an uprising project. And since Turkey is a part of NATO, and the representative of the West in the region, this will have been destroyed and marginalized, rather than attracting the world's attention towards it, but it has been denounced terribly. But there is always the ground for the revolution in Kurdistan, given the martyrs who gave their lives, and the thousands who are in prison. For example, in 2006, the great march of the people of Boutan was every day. Thousands were in the streets every day, it was a revolution. The Kurdish people are the revolution itself.

- Within the framework of these existing revolutions in the region, which are the revolutions of the people as you said, but we see political parties appearing themselves as oppositions to authoritarian regimes, how do you see the status of those parties and the oppositions involved within these revolutions?

In our vision, the revolution is divided into two parts, so that it is not misunderstood. The revolutions that take place as we said: they are the product of history, and the main player in it is the people, it is the people who take to the street, and risks themselves for the sake of their freedom, and who enters prisons, especially those young people who lead these revolutions, and in many countries women also are doing an effective role, which created this revolutionary atmosphere is the people. As for the political parties that have been around for years, they have organization, and toil, and they want to take advantage of these conditions. There are secular and religious parties, that is, they cannot absorb the people in all sides. Originally, the opposition is the force that comes to the street, and this power is the youth and women, who represent the essence of society, and they are the true owners of the revolution, and to the extent that political parties meet the demands of young people and the revolution it takes its place, and its legitimacy from the people who are considered the real owners of the revolution.

- are there parties and personalities that move towards the revolution only for the sake of its authoritarian interests and dreams? If it is, how can they impose their existence?

Of course, there is, for example, the Brotherhood movement that seizes opportunities. In all countries, necessarily, there is a rejection of the people toward the ruling regime, and here the common denominators between these opportunists and the oppressed people converge, and since the parties have organization outside and inside, they benefit from the revolution in order to follow and take advantage of the conditions, and reach power, in Egypt it was, Tunisia, and in Libya also we saw the same thing ...

- Now there are many opinions and analyzes that say that these revolutions are (external conspiracies) , and these (conspiracies) are aimed at dividing the region again. What do you think of that? Are revolutions nothing but conspiracies?

This is not true, because the one who follows this theory is the regime itself, and those close to it, and those who have no interest in the revolution; Because the revolution appears as a result of the need, and a rejection of the reality of living, if today thousands of people take to the streets, and they confront tanks and cannons with their chest, then this proves the justice of the revolution and the legitimacy of the demands of society. Yes, there are conspiracies and plans being hatched abroad, but this cannot make us deny the reality of the popular revolution, and the demands of the peoples for their freedom.

- Western powers seek to have a role in these revolutions, as is the case in Libya and other countries. How do you see the role of Western powers in these revolutions? Let's ask the question in another way: to what extent can external forces save these revolutions in their interests, and how far can they conduct them according to their strategies?

All of these regimes currently in existence from Tunisia to Syria and others are all built according to the style that Western countries wanted, that is, the model of the nation-state. It is the product of capitalism. These regimes that lead these countries (in the region) are one of the products of that mentality. The regimes created by the world order previously have reached a point where they cannot serve globalization and global forces, as happened in Iraq; Therefore, world powers had to take advantage of these conditions to change regimes, and define them in a way that serves their interests and what the new phase requires. The world powers started that project from Iraq, but they stopped after that, and did not continue, meaning that the world powers wanted to bring about a change in these regimes even before these revolutions, and with the spark of the revolutions launched, they had the opportunity again. On the other hand, the peoples of the Middle East are tired of these regimes, and this was a common denominator between those world powers and oppressed peoples, and therefore a rapprochement occurred between them. We see this as normal, perhaps Western powers want to take revenge on the regimes that they fought against, such as Libya and Syria. The Western world powers do not want the Middle East to get out of its control, Therefore, they only want to change the authority according to their interests, and does not take the will of the people as a basis for this in their calculations. These forces do not want the people of the Middle East to be cut off from the tail of the policies of the world order, and live within their social reality, therefore they strive to make some reforms in the pyramid of power without society, and re-create their interests, and examples in Tunisia and Egypt are good evidence of this.

These revolutions will change its status, but not in the form and hopes they want, but it will also be a tool for Western powers. That is, there will be a consensus between these two ideas, that is, between the people's revolution and the endeavors of world powers. But people will take much more positive steps toward freedom and democracy than before.

- What about Turkey, it also wants to be a player in these revolutions. Turkey, which was previously heading towards Europe, but when these revolutions were launched, it seems as if it has turned its direction and is working to show itself as if it is in support of these revolutions, and wants to be a model for these countries where revolutions occur?

Turkey has an important role in the region, and it gain importance from its seriousness, and who does not understand Turkey's role in the region will enter the revolution in a state of danger. Turkey has been employed by world powers to fulfill the role entrusted to it in the region, as it has been employed before; In order to put the former regimes under its control, it was therefore approaching the Syrian, Libyan regimes and others, But when the revolutions began, Turkey has supported them, and more precisely it supports Islamic movements in these revolutionary countries, not on the basis of their support, but on the basis of subjugating them under its control and conducting them according to Western interests. People want to change these old regimes, and the Western powers also want that, as Turkey changed its role according to these developments. And the most dangerous aspect of its role; It wants - since it took the lead role - to impose its model on those countries, and restore

its old Ottoman dream through that role, and in another way it wants to show itself as the ideal model that must be applied in the region.

From the Syrian side, for example; Turkey approached the Syrian state, especially after the Adana agreement in 1998, and Turkey considered Syria as one of its provinces, especially from the economic side. Today, when the decision was taken to change the Syrian regime, Turkey is now seeking to do this through the Syrian revolution, and with it will conduct Western interests also. Turkey's dangerous role lies here. Of course, this does not take place easily. For example, in Egypt the matter was different Egypt confronted and rejected the Turkish role, because Egypt represents a great civilization, and Libya also did not fully follow the Turkish model, so this will not be easy for Turkey and others.

- There are some Arab countries, especially the Gulf states, and although their rule is royal, and there are no elections, and the people who revolt today revolt against this mentality, yet these countries show themselves as supportive of these revolutions in terms of media and economic, and show that they Garrison of the Middle East revolutions? To what truth is this idea based?

We can say that there is a sharing of work and interests in the Middle East. The Gulf states want to play their part, and have done so. Turkey plays its role militarily, as it is a strong country in terms of organization and organizes the Islamic ideology, while the Gulf countries, plays its role in terms of media and economic. These countries have their functions and roles, which are set by the world powers, to take the lead of these revolutions. Qatar supports the revolution through Al-Jazeera, and Saudi Arabia through Al-Arabiya channel, all of which play an effective role in these revolutions. On the other hand, since these countries are economically strong, they also support the revolutions financially. But it is impossible for these countries to become a model for peoples. Because they rule their countries through monarchy they exchange power by inheritance within the same family. And the revolution of peoples is essentially against this mentality. Global powers cannot control the Gulf states more than this, so they give them the role to control other countries through them. In Bahrain, for example, the opposition advanced a lot, and it was suppressed by the military side, especially by (the shield of the island), because the global powers gave it legitimacy in that, and this shows the deception and reality of the Gulf states and world powers.

- What are the dangers for these new revolutions?

There are risks that they will be removed from their content and left meaningless. This old accumulation of peoples, especially after the map of the Middle East was drawn according to the concept of (the nation-state) after the First World War, and to this day, we see that this is the first time that the people of the Middle East have risen for their truth and history, and this may become the basis of the new civilization and it becomes an essential part of the world side by side with the West, and there is a great historical opportunity to achieve this. But there are some parties that engage with the Western powers

in bargaining in order to seize power and achieve personal interests, and this constitutes a serious obstacle in the face of revolutions, by emptying them of their content and meaning, so that these revolutions become formal. As a result, these revolutions, which represent the will of the peoples of the Middle East, will bring with them a major change, and will be a historical shift, meaning that the peoples after the revolution will not be as they were before the revolution, but will come very close to freedom, justice and democracy. Whatever happens, peoples will take a historic step, and they will enter a new stage.

- What are the factors that guarantee the success of these revolutions and their success in reaching their goals?

From this side we should not make mistakes in the estimates. That is, the strength and will of the people must be trusted. Many take Egypt model as an example. They say: "The Egyptian revolution did not change, and the army that is now running the state is doing what Mubarak was doing, and nothing has changed." This view is wrong, But for these revolutions not to reach only a partial result, and in order to achieve all of their goals in freedom and democracy, they must always depend on the strength and will of the people. And that the revolution is always in a state of continuity and development, and not to stop at a certain point. Let us take the Libyan model as an example. The revolution succeeded, and the people live in freedom more than before, but because they relied on NATO and external forces, they are now compelled to implement the conditions of those forces that they allied with during the revolution, and they are forced to achieve the interests of the West, and this what makes reaching the goals of the revolution relative.

Therefore, for a revolution to become a real revolution, it must rely only on itself and its people. Consequently, the people must organize themselves so that all segments of society take their place in the revolution and in the process of building a new system. Only with this mechanism can the revolution achieve its goals. In other words, If this revolution wants to reach its goals, then it must have a comprehensive and broad reform program. The goal of the revolution is not only to change the head of the regime, since the change must be radical; That is, changing the mentality on which that regime was founded, and this requires a very broad program through direct democracy that includes all groups of society and its segments.

- In many countries where revolutions have erupted and their dictatorships have been shattered, such as Egypt, Tunisia and Libya, there are ongoing discussions about forming a new government and authority and looking for its shape, mechanisms, and powers. What is the pattern required for the imagined government to fulfill the goals of the revolution in your opinion?

In my view, the change of power does not lie in the people, and perhaps the new people who will come to power can make some changes in the authoritarian mentality, and achieve few achievements, but this will not last long until the authority returns as it was before. Whatever the form of power, it will not change anything radically, if there is a socialist power, a liberal and a nationalist power, but they did not make any fundamental change. The programs of other reformist parties, and secular parties, are not very different from the existing regimes, so this is not the ideal pattern for achieving the goals of the revolution. But the ideal form that we see is building a social democratic system, so that society as a whole becomes a power. We do not want a democratic authority; We want a democratic society. For example: It is now said that there is a revolution, and there are parties, the strongest party, more organized, and more supportive, and who has more money, will control Parliament, then it will be alone in power, establish a government, and run society and the state. This is not the ideal type, but rather the ideal model that we say about (the real revolution); It is a democratic society, which is represented through self-administration, not through a parliament that represents the people, but rather the people can manage themselves locally, and this is what society wants in order to be democratic and just.

- The political Islam model that is now being discussed among some parties. Can this model be an answer that meets the requirements of the people and succeeds in leading the community?

Political Islam wants to take advantage of these conditions, it is compatible with world order, and it wants to play the role that nationalist regimes were playing, and thus this does not constitute anything different from those nationalist regimes that used to govern in the past. What the Baath was doing in Iraq and Syria, the parties of political Islam want to take on the role of these repressive regimes. And of course they were taken into account and assigned a role to them by world powers in light of these changes. The most powerful example of political Islam is Turkey, in particular through the Justice and Development Party.

It is impossible for this model to be desired by peoples, because freedom and democracy are narrowed under these regimes, and society is being managed worse than it is now.

- Most of the authoritarianists against whom revolutions were held came mainly to power through (revolutions) and coups, and some of them were the leader of a revolution? What happened to become enemies of the revolution and their people revolt against them?

They themselves called these opportunistic movements and military coups as (revolutions), in fact that was just personal goals seeking to reach the seat of power, and they convinced the people that they were accomplishing historical revolutions. Some of them came through military coups, some with a group of people revolted with them, others came from the nationalist thought that exists among the peoples of the region, and they promised that they would solve the problems and national complexity in the Middle East, and the people also placed hopes on them and hoped for good from them. for example; The movement of Gamal Abdel Nasser, which occurred in 1952 and which was called (the July 23 Revolution), and that movement was justified, which was originally a military coup within the army and led by the army against the regime; And since it was (hostility to external forces), the Egyptian people, indeed the entire Arab nation, stood behind (the Nasserist revolution), and he in turn called for Arab national unity, and he gained a position among the Arab people. But he basically did not achieve anything from the interests of society, there was no fundamental change that would enable the society to run itself, the people could not develop through its internal energy. He established authority over the will of the people, established a nation-state, and no fundamental change occurred, so he could not solve the problems of society, nor did he achieve the slogans he used to launch and based on its noise, which are "freedom and democracy." He did not develop anything, and was not cut off from world powers, but rather moved within the network of external interests. From inside, he did not solve the class divide in society, but rather wanted to run society through a certain class, then administered it from one class, and with the passage of time the class became just a family, and the result became the rule of a small minority in the face of society Entire. And he gradually moved away from his reality. Or rather, he did not depart from his truth originally, but his truth appeared in front of everyone, when he was able to organize himself and formed a basis for him, his truth was revealed. This mentality persists to this day. This is the path in which all the regimes of the Middle East entered, starting with the Egyptian revolution, then what the Baath did in Syria and Iraq, and what Gaddafi did, they represent one truth; It is the bourgeoisie and nationalist thought, and in this way they have won the people for some time in terms of nationalist slogans and sentiments, but this was not in essence a real revolution, nor a new thing, and they did not represent society, but they claimed that; Because they were a power that governed society through a certain class that moved away from society.. Today the same scenario is repeated, as one party tried to control society and make power a target for it, for example there is (the Iranian revolution), that revolution was not only Khomeini's revolution, but the entire people's revolution for freedom and democracy, and in the result only power changed and the reign of power has moved from the authority of the Shah to the authority of the mullahs, and nothing has changed in essence. Before the revolution, the Persian nationalist ideology was the dominant one, and after the revolution the Persian Shi'a ideology became the dominant one. And they wanted to develop Shia nationalism. The Iranian regime has become more tyrannical than before, has lost its moral side, has run the community with strength and injustice, and Khomeini's truth has emerged for everyone; That is, he has not changed after the revolution, but this is his reality.

The bottom line lies in the following process: at first they come close to society, and after they organize themselves and have power, they form their gangs and classes, then they oppose to society, and they subjugate it under their control.

- In your talk, you often refer to the (nation-state) , and you refer to its failure to lead society. What is the reason behind the failure of the (nation-state) in the Middle East, in your opinion? How can we neglect and deny national thought?

There have always been two forces in the history of human civilization, a force that represents the will of an ethical democratic society, and the power of a state system based on authoritarianism and class. Authoritarian power represents a small segment of society, and society as a whole is not represented. Since the establishment of the Sumerian state and until that authoritarian layer continues, no matter how that authority wants to change its form, in the end nothing in society will change, let alone whether it is in the feudal state, the socialist state, or the capitalist state. The nation-state that was established with capitalist modernity, and which leaked into the countries of the Middle East in the most brutal and tyrannical form, is artificial and has nothing in its essence. Where the nation-state claims to represent the whole of society;

Like the Ba'ath Party and the Qaddafi regime, it has a totalitarian character, but in the end, they represent only a part of society, not all of it. And with the passage of time this segment becomes a small minority more and more. As we mentioned earlier: to be confined to one family. Most Middle Eastern regimes are like this the rule of one family. Originally, the rule of one family is not different from the nation-state, because it is one of its secretions, and there are hundreds of similar examples in the world.

These existing revolutions will weaken (the mentality of the nation-state), but if they do not change in their essence anything, then power will be in the hands of one party and represent a certain class of society, and authoritarianism and class will continue. Whatever the party's structure and ideology, be it social, socialist or otherwise, nothing will change. For example, the experience that took place in southern Kurdistan, it is a beautiful and useful thing for the Kurds to appear as a nation and an independent people from the economic, social and other aspects, but this does not represent all the requirements of the Kurds, because there are two parties that rule, and now there are family differences for governance, this is not represents society in southern Kurdistan as a whole. As if the same scenario of the nation-state that we mentioned earlier continues in the Kurdistan region in its phases; Initially a revolution took place in the name of all the Kurdish people, then two parties ruled there, and now the decision is confined to the one family. The revolution there needs to be reformed.

- let us return to the first question and follow up from there. Where we had started our conversation by defining the revolution; If we say the revolution is a verb, we must refer to the revolutionary as a subject. Today, all people call themselves revolutionaries. In your opinion, who is the revolutionary? What are the characteristics of a revolutionary person?

As we said earlier, the revolution change society, not power and governance. When the obstacles are removed in front of society, society begins to breathe freely, and expresses its will by itself, and the way is opened for the natural development of society. This is called a revolution. The revolution does not mean the removal of a person, family or a segment, but rather a change of mentality. The revolution has a comprehensive concept that is long discussed. As for who is the revolutionary person? We see that the revolutionary is the sacrifice person. And the revolutionary is the one who cuts all ties to the regime in his philosophy, life, principles, and daily practices. True revolutionaries give meaning to everything, and live accordingly. For all the values imposed by capitalist modernity, the revolutionaries sever their relations with that regime in all social and material terms completely. In our concept; who receives his salary from the state is impossible to be revolting, even Marx was linked to the regime in all side, because he did not cut off his relationship with the existing regime at the time. As for the real revolutionary, he cut off from all aspects of the political, social and economic state, as there is no connection with the state. So the revolution carries a comprehensive and broad meaning that we cannot deny, as some of them attend in the institutions of the regime, receive their salary from it, and at the same time demand to be dropped. Such people can be supporters of the revolution, and support the revolution on one side or the other, but they cannot be revolutionaries Some have given a superficial and insignificant meaning to the revolution, and we must fight attempts to trivial the meaning of revolution. For example, if there is a movement linked to external forces, and it receives its support from the outside in all military and economic aspects, it cannot be called a revolution, because it does not depend on itself.

What happened in Libya cannot be described as a revolution; Because it relied entirely on the outside. Perhaps we find that there is a popular aspect to it, and it is somewhat different from the old authority, but it is a new authority linked to abroad. Consequently, the people who were fighting were not real revolutionaries either, because they did not hold a different mindset from the regime they were revolting against.

Those who demand the downfall of the regime in Syria, but at the same time are not ready to cut all ties with this regime, because schools and universities are running normally, and employees go to their departments. They are not ready to sacrifice what they have and therefore they are not revolutionaries, yes they are patriots, and they love the revolution, but they are not revolutionaries. It was at this time that the revolution and revolutionaries fashion came out. Not everyone demanding the downfall of the regime is considered revolting, we should not take this superficially. That is, they are tied from their toes and even their noses to the regime, and they do not want to sacrifice the life that these despotic regimes have made for them, so those are not revolutionaries. The revolutionary is not by slogans, but the revolutionary is the free man who cut all his ties with the regime

-There are mass revolutions or mass movements that succeeded peacefully, as happened in Tunisia and Egypt, but in the Libyan case and the Syrian case, we note that they are now heading towards the military option to resolve the matter. What are the negative effects that could affect the revolution and its future results? Is the military option possible within the revolution?

The revolution's resort to violence, may be the result of the need or the response of counter-violence and compelling pressure. But this must be legitimate, and self-defense must be used. Therefore, it is not necessary that the revolution be peaceful. No, this is not a condition. When you need to protect yourself, your defense will be legitimate. But when you use only the armed side, and do not give importance to the other aspects, this brings with it the negative effects most likely; Because when the armed revolution comes out of the concept of (self-defense), it becomes illegal. In the event that the armament is linked to the outside, then the one who armed you will be primarily due to his interests, and thus the situation will go towards vandalism. We value the legitimacy and illegality of armaments in the context of self-defense primarily.

- In the midst of the process of the people or the opposition seeking to overthrow the regime, and in the event that it resorted to (inhuman) methods that guarantee its success in its goals, is that permissible in such cases, from the perspective of "the end justifies the means"?

There are examples from history. When violence is misplaced, it brings great harm. To give the example of the Soviet state; When violence was used, especially in Stalin's time on the pretext of protecting the Soviet power, this became one of the most important reasons for its eventual downfall. But when the people depend on themselves and establish a force for their own protection, this is legitimate, natural and positive, but through the examples that we see, all revolutions depend on the outside and therefore repeat the same mistakes of the authorities.

- In light of these revolutions and the changes that are taking place, there are components that live in those countries such as the Amazighs, Kurds, Armenians, Copts, Christians, Circassians and other religious minorities or national and ethnic components. Can these revolutions and changes be in the interest of these minorities as well and benefit from them?

Of course there will be benefit, because this is a popular movement, and there will be changes in terms of respecting minorities, and giving them some advantages. But when the revolution does not carry an integrated and comprehensive program, achieving its goal will be relative as in Egypt, which needs to continue its revolution. And in Syria, they are trying to reduce the revolution to toppling power, and in one person, and they say that they will solve everything later, and this is wrong, because the revolution must be accompanied by a comprehensive and broad program on freedom, democracy, and the rights of minorities and components without discrimination.

- In the Egyptian experience, we noticed an objection and constraint against the Christian Copts. Also, Christians in Syria are afraid of repeating the same thing with them. Those who are at the forefront of the Syrian revolution today say: "This is not the time for the minorities." It is said to the Kurds: "Silence now so that you do not influence the true course of the revolution." Do minorities have to fear for themselves?

This discourse rises from the mentality of power and the narrow nationalist state. Previously, the Baath Party used to say: "We must leave everything now, and direct all our energies towards Palestine and the Palestinian cause." Others say the same thing today, this is the mentality of power. But they must know that the revolution is a popular revolution, so the revolution must be the owner of a program that fulfills all the interests of the people. Including religious and national minorities, and every class, sect, and nationality will participate in the revolution with its identity and privacy, and a comprehensive program for the revolution will be established, as the revolution is not slogans. They said the same thing in the Iranian revolution: "Let's do the revolution and reach Islamic rule, then we will solve all our issues." They said: "We will overthrow the rule of the Shah at the beginning, build an Islamic state, expel the Shah, and all agree later." And when the Shah fell, the various minorities and components did not benefit from anything, but their conditions worsened more and more, and their struggle is still continuing until now, and they have not benefited from that revolution. In the Iranian revolution, the struggle was in the name of (Islam), and now in Syria in the name of (one country, targeting power).

- Leaders of the revolution are now seeking to topple and execute the president. Do you think that this revolution will reach this goal and then stop and announce its victory? Is this the (sacred) goal of the revolution?

The revolution that takes the will of peoples as its foundation; Compelled to make a fundamental change in the structure of the regime, and in the end there is a person who represents the regime, and this regime is supported by a certain class, so the regime does not change by changing that person, but the entire mentality of that segment must be changed, and as we said that changing the regime in itself is not enough and change is not limited to changing a person or changing the pillars of the state only. Here lies our difference from the mentality of these existing revolutions. We want to change the whole authoritarian regime in order to establish in his place a different societal system, in other words, and fundamentally, there must be a democratic society system alternative to the authoritarian state regime.

- Do you see that the goal is a fundamental change in society or a change in the prevailing relationships in form and content?

Change must not be confined to the head of the authority and its departments or institutions, but rather to changing the whole authoritarian mentality. For example, there is a legislative authority, or what is said: (People's Assembly), but in the end it represents one or two parties, and at the same time the most popular party is the one that controls society, and thus controls the state, and the one party does not represent the interests of all society. On the other hand, there is the military power that protects the state, the government, and the authority, and does not protect society So it exists to protect power only. At that time, the community must build its institutions away from the authority of the state, and the state may exist (for its function to coordinate the work of the society, to organize it without its rule, and not to overpower it) and the institutions that are built; must be built from the base, and not from the top, all institutions must be reorganized according to this form, and therefore the departments of those institutions will serve as the general coordinator of society. Then the mentality of society will change in form and substance.

- It seems that you agree with the other parties that this regime should leave, and fall because it is authoritarian and repressive, but there is a reservation by you not to raise the slogan of "overthrowing the regime", what is the reason for your reservation?

If you want the truth, we want to overthrow the regime more than everyone else, but if there is a new authority that will come to power without a comprehensive program and a specific goal, this (the overthrow) will not change anything, and those who repeat (we want to overthrow the regime) actually want to replace Power, they want the power for themselves. Our vision says that the authority should leave, and not return again - the same as the nation-state - and be replaced by the democratic society's system of administration. Therefore, we prefer to build all our institutions from the grassroots until we reach a point where the state does not have any meaning and then it falls! That is, we can say: there are two powers in nature; One of them; The authority of society itself, and the other is the authority of the state. It is important for the state's authority to weaken, and in return, to strengthen the power of a naturally developing democratic society. The organization of society is the guarantee of freedom and democracy for all, and this is the major social force in which the power of the state and the power of one clique or one person are lacking. In other words, we are building a society through which the regime's power is steadily diminishing until it falls.

- This power and the existing regime are the main obstacle to the lack of development or application of that philosophy, that is, the philosophy of a democratic society. Don't you see that the fall of the regime (first) provides an opportunity for society to play this role? For example you put forward several projects years ago to organize society on a democratic basis, but the might of the regime was an obstacle in front of you at that time, and now the regime has weakened, and you are implementing your project, don't you see that the fall of the regime will allow the community to develop faster and better?

When we call slogans, and the regime falls, another authority will come to replace it, and nothing will change. But when we establish a ground for the progress of society, the regime is slowly weakening, and the meaning of the regime's survival or fall does not make sense, it will effectively fall. Then the ruling authority will not only fall, but the dominance of authoritarian mentality over society is removed. Of course we want to overthrow the regime, but within a comprehensive program, so that a democratic society is the alternative, so the alternative must be ready, strong.

We must not forget that there are special conditions and circumstances for a revolution in the Middle East. We always say: the revolution must have clear goals, a clear program, and community building will be the basis. But if the goal of the revolution is to bring down only the head of power, and put everything aside, and say: "We will solve other issues later", its meaning will not be a revolution, and its goal will not be achieved.

As for us, the Kurds, we have our privacy, and I say it very frankly: Our priorities are our rights above all. The job of the Kurds is not to overthrow the regimes in Damascus, Tehran, Ankara, and Baghdad, but rather the job of the Kurds is to work for their rights in Qamishlo, Mahabad, Amad, and Hawler. And if the topple oblige the Kurds, then we will bring down those forces that divided the Kurdish people, and worked on melting and denying them.

-You often speak sharply and critically about the state and the authority, and that it does not work. What is the reason for that?

We have many experiences in history, and experiences were inspired from the history of other peoples as well, for example; Often efforts go to waste, as revolutions are made against the tyrant, and thousands of sacrifices are made, but the result is the same as before, and the rotation is in the same blank circle. To give an example of these regimes that the people seek to bring down, they had come to power through revolutions before, and some of them made sacrifices, and the people were with them during that, but in the end the revolution became power, and it did not serve the people or society, and now the people want to falling off it!. Another article on the socialist revolution that millions of people participated in and millions of sacrifice presented for major goals, but in the end they fell into repeating the same practices that they revolted against. That is why we have come to the conviction that building an alternative authority to an authority, or a state rather than a state, will have no benefit. But this does not mean that there is no alternative, but rather that it has an alternative, which is building an ecological democratic society, and thus society reaches its freedom, this is what we depend on in our revolution. If the thing that we want is to build society and remove obstacles in front of it, then we must create our own self-defense system to protect ourselves, then the war will be, and the struggle will make sense. In other words, what distinguish our struggle is that we build the alternative, and we drop the regime together. This is our theory and on the basis of which we struggle.

- Everyone has recently called for freedom and democracy, America is calling for democracy, regime and opposition, and Turkey are calling for it ... Democracy has become a popular fashion these days. You also call for democracy, but how does your democracy differ from the democracy of others?

Democracy has become a universal requirement, and everyone wants it, and calls for it, but the interpretation of the concept of democracy differs among all, we can say: There are two types of democracies; There is a representative democracy, and there is a people's democracy. And we are not with a representative democracy, that is, there are some people who speak in the name of society. This is not democracy. For example, the American people are forced to choose every four years one of the two parties, that is to choose between two people; One is Democratic and the other is

Republican; There is no other option for the people or a substitute for them. Also, the parliamentary system in the whole world is like this, with one or two parties controlling Parliament and claiming to represent the people. We are against that concept. The democracy we are demanding is direct democracy, a people's democracy, whose decisions and representations start from the basis to the top, the democracy of the councils. It is made up of village councils, neighborhoods, and all segments of society who make their own decisions. That is, the community in all its categories, and its segments are present in the council, and decisions are issued from them.

- Within the movement of the peoples 'spring, we see the rise of the Arab people against their authoritarian regimes, as well as the rise of the Kurdish people against the repressive regimes, but until this moment this spring did not knock on the gates of Iran. Why the Iranian people did not rise?

If you want the truth, the Iranian people revolted before everyone else and launched their revolution repeatedly, but that revolution was destroyed. Two years ago, the people revolted against that ruling regime, but the oppression and strength of the regime, the strength of its institutions and the strength of its Islamic ideology hindered and aborted the revolution. I think that the peoples 'spring will inevitably reach Iran, so Iran is working to strengthen its relations with Syria, Turkey and the Lebanese forces and take its precautionary measures. The Iranian people are part of this spring. We also do not forget the existence of the Kurdish issue in Iran as well, which is an important issue, and the Kurdish struggle is advancing there, although the Iranian regime is trying to abort that struggle through executions and oppression. We are confident that the Kurdish movement will play an important role in democratic change in Iran, sooner or later.

- The demonstrations took place in neighboring countries, and the protests began, for example the protests of Baghdad and southern Kurdistan, the authorities dealt severely with the demonstrators, and victims fell among them, but after a short time these protests stopped, what is the reason behind the stopping these demonstrations?

Yes, there were demonstrations and protests in Iraq, southern Kurdistan, and Turkey as well, but they stopped, there are many reasons, including the strength of the institutions of those countries, and they have justifications, for example the Iraqi authorities say to the people: "We are still in the construction phase, and we are building democracy, and we have not finished

After this process, be patient with us. " As for Kurdistan; The national side is in control, and the national issue comes before the social issue, in addition to their orientation towards some reforms. In Turkey, the authorities are merging nationalism with the religious question in its response to any anti-movement. This also happened in Bahrain world order are against such protests in these countries, and they hinder the opposition in those countries and do not give them space, and they also protect those regimes.

- So, can we say: If these world order do not support or bless, the revolutions will not succeed? the people's uprising will be futile?

No, we cannot say it will not succeed, but it will go on, it will be more difficult, and it will make many sacrifices and efforts. Here we can present the example of Yemen, which seems that America does not want the Yemeni regime to fall; Because he is a strategic ally, and an enemy of al Qaeda. There is a fall of the victims, and the blood is profusely wasted in Yemen, but the people's persistence and its millions of demonstrations will ensure the success of their revolution, and make them excel and continue despite the opposition of the world powers. Another example is northern Kurdistan, which is a similar case. The Kurdish people have a right and a just case, but most of the world order stand with the Turkish state, and everyone calls the Kurdish revolution in northern Kurdistan a (terrorism), but despite that, the Kurdish people continue to struggle heroically, and the revolution expands day by day. True, the price will be high, but the will of the people will win in the end.

THE SECOND CHAPTER

The revolution in Syria, and the positions of the Kurdish movement regarding it

- A few months ago, in mid-February of this year, protests started in many Syrian cities and expanded over time until it became a major popular revolution. Did you expect the protests to start in Syria?

Yes, immediately after the outbreak of the revolution in Tunisia our attention turned to Syria, and we were expecting the outbreak of the revolution in it. Our expectations are due to two main reasons:

The first reason is the depth of the social contradictions that exist in the country, and their accumulations over the past years, especially since such contradictions are; what led to the popular revolutions in other countries, but the situation in Syria was deeper and more severe. We were well aware that it would be the cause of the explosion and revolution in the country. Especially since Syria did not carry out the required democratic reforms, if it had done so years ago, it would be different now, but it has not. Congestion has reached an intolerable level. After the revolution in Tunisia and Egypt, the revolution and the outburst of anger are inevitable in Syria as well.

As for the second reason, everyone knows that Syria was on the list of countries that should be controlled by Western powers for years. After the Western intervention in Iraq, Syria turned more attention, but the intervention was postponed for many reasons, but this did not remove it from the circle of Western interest and did not get out of their calculations until the right opportunity came at the beginning of this year.

- What are the main reasons behind the revolution of the Syrian people against the regime in the country?

The main reason is freedom ... There is no such thing "freedom" in Syria. The regime in Syria is an authoritarian, dictatorial regime, under the control of a single party holding all aspects of life and administration in the country. All of this means the lack of freedom in the country. Also, there are many social contradictions that were born as a result of the status quo. The people suffer from many problems in the social, economic and living fields, until the people are deprived of living in the simplest form. Also, administrative corruption is suspiciously prevalent in state agencies and all administrative facilities and government departments.

All of this led to the inability of society to continue living its normal life under this regime the people want freedom and seek it. Therefore, we see slogans such as (freedom) prevail in the demonstrations of the masses in the country, because the people want their freedom and realize very well that they cannot live without it.

- The Syrian revolution has entered its seventh month, but the state and the regime, with its media, representatives, and leaders, are still talking about "external conspiracy" and "targeting the country by foreign powers" and "armed terrorist groups" and other statements and designations of the Syrian revolution. How true are these statements? Is Syria really vulnerable to an external conspiracy under the name (the revolution)?

These allegations are incorrect, and are not objective analysis. The main reason for the rise of the Syrian people is primarily due to internal affairs. As long as the state is blind to seeing this truth, and does not abandon its fossilized logic, this problem will never be solved. Linking the popular revolution to conspiracies, and the external parties are incorrect. Likewise, all solutions put in this light will be wrong, and will not be helpful in resolving issues. This is the main reason for the failure to find successful and real solutions to the issue until now. As we have previously said, the main cause of this revolution is the lack of freedoms in the country, and the suffocating pressures upon society, which exploded through this revolution.

Despite all of this, we cannot deny the external role, just as we know very well western projects regarding Syria, in order to push it to change and transform in a way that suits the strategic interests of the West. But it is internal conditions that allow these schemes to materialize or achieve.

- We all know the countries that were closest to the Syrian regime and were friendly to it, such as France, Qatar, and Turkey, as well as Russia. But we see today that these countries have turned against the Syrian regime, and have reached the point of boycotting, even hostility. What is the reason behind this coup against the regime by friends of yesterday?

In our opinion, nothing fundamentally changed. Despite the talk about the coup of these countries against Syria it does not express the essence of the truth. These countries were not friendly to Syria, for example Turkey, which has worked over the past years to put Syria under its total control in all forms. Where these countries were seeking to withdraw Syria to the melting pot of the world order through the existing regime, but today, these countries have started to run the same policy, but with a different form and style. In the aftermath of the outbreak of popular revolts against the existing regimes, and after these countries have confirmed that the Syrian people (rebelling for their freedom) will overthrow this regime, and inevitably annihilate it, and then it is certain that the people will make great changes for the sake of freedom and democracy, and many of these steps will not serve the interests of the world order. Therefore, these countries rushed to change their stances, and pretended that they are on the side of the revolutionary Syrian people, in order to circumvent the revolution and ensure that it does not exit from their initiative in the future. These forces are now seeking to achieve their previous goals through the popular revolution. This means that the analyzes that these countries have turned against, betrayed or turned away from Syria are incorrect. These countries and powers are working to plunder, exploit, and steal the Syrian revolution.

- We all know that the Kurdish people are considered the second largest nationalist in the country, and they have an important geography, and they were active participants throughout the Syrian political history, so where are the Kurdish people today from the Syrian popular revolution? What is their role? And their stature?

In fact, if we say that the Syrian revolution has begun between the Kurds and the Kurdish regions, it will not be a wrong analysis. Not seeing the Kurdish role, and its sacrifices in the Syrian revolution, will be a great injustice. Unfortunately, there are many people, and those who act in this way and deny any role to the Kurds. Many of the chauvinist parties are approaching in this way, and so are some "Kurds" who deny their truth and their national peculiarities. The Kurdish people have been and continue to be a very effective role in the process of democratic change, guaranteeing freedoms, and reform in Syria, especially since the year 2000, and these efforts reached the level of overwhelming revolution during the March 12 uprising in 2004. Where this Uprising was a major revolution in the face of the regime. It was an uprising for the freedom, democracy, and legitimate rights of the Kurdish people. However, because the world order and Turkey were hostile to the Kurdish people 's realization of any of their rights, they took the initiative to help the regime crush this revolution. Many forces, and parties that pretend today, that they support the Syrian popular revolution, have stood by the regime at the time, and accused the Kurdish masses of "conspiring and targeting national unity", and other accusations that are not true. We confirm again that the Syrian revolution started in the uprising of March 12 in 2004, and no one can deny this fact. Also, the Kurdish people did not stop from that time from 2004 to 2011, and made many sacrifices, martyrs, and detainees, but despite everything they did not retreat from the struggle for freedom and obtaining their legitimate rights. If the Syrian Arab people had risen against the regime today, the Kurdish people, and their revolutionary stand, would have the essential role in that, especially after the March 12 uprising. The Kurdish people have an important role and prestige in the Syrian popular revolution, and they cannot be overlooked or denied. As for those who seek to make the extent of the Kurdish street's participation in the path of some parties of the opposition bound under Turkish influence a measure of Kurdish participation in the revolution, this is a wrong convergence, and we cannot accept it. We will be more candid, we do not measure Kurdish people participation In the Syrian revolution to the extent of their compliance with the plans, the decisions coming from Turkey, and the extent of their service to the policy of some undemocratic parties in the foreign opposition. We do not measure them by the extent of their transformation into soldiers for the foreign agenda, or tools in the hands of opposition parties that do not accept the Kurdish presence at all. We do not consider (Kurdish) parties that engage under these conditions that they represent the reality of the Kurdish people, and they do not represent the Kurdish participation in the Syrian revolution at all. As for the real Kurdish position, it has been clear for years against this regime. today, the Kurdish people are an active participant in the revolution, for the sake of democratic transformation in Syria, the attainment of their freedom, and their legitimate national rights. And because the Kurdish people contribute to this revolution with its national identity and national characteristics, some parties do not want to see this as a participation in the revolution. But we do not look at the issue from this perspective.

- The Syrian revolution has entered its seventh month, after seven months of protests. Do you see that it has reached the status and strength to prepare it to win?

Attitudes varied as a result of these months, and two views appeared clearly with the opposition. The first view is that without external interference and military support, as happened in Libya, victory will not be possible for the revolution.

We do not consider this as a revolution, even something like this happens, we will not consider it a Syrian revolution, but rather it will be merely a transfer of power by the hands of external powers. As for the other view or opinion: which sees the necessity of succeeding in the revolution by relying on a peaceful method, and based on the self-power of the people. The forces representing this outlook began to expand, gain strength, and many forces took it seriously, but we see that they have not yet reached the required level of strength and influence. If the parties of internal opposition unite, and strengthen more, then it will be able to lead the revolution to a certain victory.

- How do you see the parties of the opposition? What are your conditions for working with them?

The Syrian opposition was not clear-cut at the beginning of the revolution, and it was not known and publicized about its positions yet, so we were not able at that time to pass public analyzes, and we were not able to express explicit positions towards it. Also, we had put two conditions in front of all the opposition parties; The first condition: the necessity of a real transformation of democracy, and the guarantee of freedoms in Syria, while emphasizing a fundamental change of regime, and not only the change of power. The second condition: It was about Kurdish rights. Kurdish rights are a red line for us. As the days progressed, and the revolution extended in time, the fact of the parties of the opposition were clearly visible, and its reality became clear to us.

Today, we can talk about the Syrian opposition very clearly. The Syrian opposition is divided into two main parts. The first part is the external opposition, or that is dependent on the outside, and expects them to intervene, and believes that change in Syria will only be through external intervention, and it believes in violence and a military solution, and depends mainly on Turkey, as it aims to power in the first place, Sectarian tendencies are used in this way, this spectrum of external opposition is organized within the so-called National Council in Turkey. The second part of the opposition is the internal opposition, which draws its strength from the people, and believes in democratic means to make the required transformation in Syria. It also stood against three trends: external interference, violence and sectarianism. We see it as the true opposition, and this parties of opposition are organized in the form of the Coordination Body for Democratic Change. We adopt the position of the internal opposition.

- Do you have a relationship and link with one of the parties of the Syrian opposition? What are the principles and foundations of this relationship, if any?

We are not against any of the parties of the opposition in essence, and we will not stand against any of the part of the opposition aimed at making the required change in the country. And we did not specify our position from the parties of the opposition and its trends, our doors are open to internal opposition, as well as to external opposition. But we have our terms, and principles to have a relationship with either, the prerequisite is; The Kurdish issue, the second condition; It is building a democratic system by peaceful means, and by relying on the popular forces without relying on the outside. But for the time being we see that the opposition in Ankara does not accept the recognition of Kurdish national rights, not only in Syria and western Kurdistan, but also in northern Kurdistan and Turkey as well, based on its interests and its interest to gain Turkish consent, as it accuses the Kurdish movement of (terrorist) It condemns all defensive action it takes against the excesses of the Turkish army, and calls it (terrorist operations).

This opposition speaks of freedom on the one hand, and at the same time it attacks the Kurdish struggle for freedom, and abuses the Kurdish people to enjoy freedom, on the one hand it claims that it is against oppression, persecution and injustice, but at the same time it praises Turkish repression towards our people in north Kurdistan (Bakur). Therefore, it is not possible to accept an opposition in this way, an opposition that adopts the Machiavellian logic in looking at things, as it sees all ways and methods permitted to overthrow this regime, and it does not matter if foreign countries interfere, blood is spilled in the country, or thousands of innocent victims die Therefore, as long as the external opposition affiliated with the National council does not correct its positions on these two points, we will not accept them. Of course, this does not mean that we will not talk to them, our dialogue will be continuous, but we will be against its negative positions. As for the internal opposition, we accept it, and we consider it the third force alongside both the external opposition and power. We see the internal opposition represented by the National Coordination Body as the most successful way to a peaceful and democratic solution, and it represents the true strength of the opposition. We believe that all the parties of internal opposition, from left-wing and democratic nationalist parties, and national figures alongside the Kurdish people will be the basic nucleus for building a democratic nation, and true unity between the Kurdish and Arab people; Therefore, we support the coordination body and will do everything we can to make it the main force on the ground.

- You talked about parties of opposition that do not accept Kurdish identity, and do not recognize the national rights of the Kurdish people. What are the reasons behind this denial of the Kurdish people and their rights?

The main reason is that they do not march according to the reality of the Syrian people and their aspirations for freedom, but rather they march according to external interests and plans. They have turned into tool for foreign powers that seek to take advantage of the Syrian popular revolution in order to change the regime. Some parties of the opposition realize this, and have surrendered completely to achieve their goals by relying on external forces. We realize that there is no solution to the Kurdish issue in northern and western Kurdistan within the agenda of international powers, and this is directly reflected in the positions of opposition forces embedded in the arms of the outside. Let's be more honest, as many foreign opposition forces are present in Turkey, and they follow Turkish policy on the Kurdish issue. We have certain information that the Turkish authorities have imposed on this opposition to accept the (Adana Agreement), and the last accepted it, and that it has even extended more than the Syrian regime. We have seen the repercussions of this on the ground, and the evidence does not leave any doubt about the validity of this information. This opposition has accepted all the conditions of the Turkish state, foremost of which is the Adana Agreement. Everyone knows that this agreement is primarily hostile to the Kurdish people and its liberation struggle. Hostility towards some parties of opposition to the Kurdish issue is aimed at obtaining satisfaction and Turkish support.

- There are some parties and forces that call for upholding the Syrian identity above all other identities, especially at the expense of the national identity of the Kurdish people. These parties argue that now is not the time for the Kurdish issue, and that the Kurdish nationalist demands will harm the Syrian revolution, and to the other arguments ... So should the Kurdish people really set aside their demands and abandon their national identity as a sacrifice for the Syrian identity, and as a sacrifice from it for the revolution to

succeed? Is the success of the Syrian revolution linked to the Kurds giving up their demands while the revolution is victorious? and every sessions has a different discussion then what do you think?

This express a narrow nationalist view, does not differ from the logic and mentality of the Baath, and express a chauvinist approach. There is no justification, and we cannot find any justification for denying the rights of nationalities in the name of the revolution. But the opposite is completely true. For the revolution to triumph, and to be crowned with success and victory, it must first of all be a just revolution, a democratic revolution. In any revolution there is no place for Kurdish rights and identity, it is not a democratic or just revolution, and in any revolution that does not see the Kurds right to freedom, the concept of freedom for this revolution will be incomplete and distorted. Therefore, these slogans and voices calling for the need for the Kurds to give up their rights are nothing but deceptive voices, aimed at deceiving the Kurdish people, and we are sure that the Kurdish people will not be fooled by these voices and calls and will never accept them.

- But not only the Arab opposition, but there are also Kurdish parties and figures who call for this ...

They are also partners with the parties of the undemocratic opposition. Yes, there are people who claim this ignorantly, or out of good intentions, and must be awakened. But those who do so knowingly, we say that they are betraying the Kurdish issue. Everyone who says that the solution to the Kurdish issue should be postponed until after the revolution, and they call on the Kurdish people to struggle, sacrifice for the sake of others, and neglect the Kurdish issue, they betray the Kurdish issue, and they have no Kurdish obsession, and they have nO relationship with the Kurdish people. These people can say about themselves that they are only Syrian forces, then they are not entitled to talk about the Kurdish issue, nor are they entitled to place the Kurdish street under the service of other powers. opposite to that, double standard will be in itself, on the one hand they say about themselves as Kurds, and on the other hand they call for sacrificing the Kurdish cause for the interests of other powers. Any opposition does not accept Kurdish identity and rights, and it has not yet reached power, so what if they come to power then, what will they do?! For this opposition, which is still forming itself, is weak, small, and without powers, yet it does not accept the recognition of the Kurdish people and their national rights. What will be its position when it has its strength, its army, and its institutions, so how will it accept Kurdish rights then? It would be foolish to swallow these tricks, or a traitor if he does so knowingly.

- In the last ten years, the hostility between you and the Syrian regime has reached a very high level, and the attacks of the regime against you have been most severe, as hundreds of your cadres, thousands of your activists, and your supporters have been arrested, hundreds of them are still in prison, and many Kurds militants have also been delivered to the Turkish authorities, and killed many of them in the basements and prisons, and it never hesitate to target you. But today, many observers are talking about harmony between you and this regime, and many parties suspect that you have relations with the state and accuse you of all kinds of accusations. What do you say in this regard?

The true source of these rumors, accusations and allegations is the Turkish state and its special war departments. It claims that we and the Syrian regime have agreed against Turkey. There are many parties, and people in Syria and western Kurdistan repeat the statements of the Turkish media and their special war department. We know very well who is behind it, who prepares it, publishes it, and markets these false rumors. And I will say that there is no harmony between us and the Syrian regime, and hundreds of our comrades are still in its prisons, and this regime has recently handed over many cadres to the Turkish authorities, that is, during the current events. We have certain information about dozens of secret visits of Turkish authorities to Syria to agree on putting plans against us, and there are talks and malicious deals between the two countries aimed at fighting us The only thing that changed in the matter, is that the regime is no longer kidnapping, arresting, and killing our comrades. Is it our destiny to be killed, to be arrested, and to always die, does this have to be our destiny always? There are those who say that "the fighter in our movement, if he is not killed, has not been executed, has not been kidnapped, and has not been arrested, then there is something wrong." They tell us, "Why don't you die?

Why don't you be executed? And why are you out of prison?" We know very well that the current policy of the Syrian regime towards the Kurdish areas and the Kurdish people revolve around not stirring them, and not fighting them directly. Therefore, the state applies a balanced and sensitive policy towards all Kurds without exception. We all see that the Kurds demonstrate against the regime in the streets of Amouda and Qamishlo, and they call for the overthrow of the regime, the execution of Bashar, and they destroy the statues of Hafez al-Assad, and raise all slogans against the regime, but the regime does not do anything against them, and does not interfere in dispersing their demonstrations except rarely. This matter stems from a special policy of the state towards the Kurdish people in general, and we are also part of the Kurdish people, part of the political movement, and we benefit, like other from the new conditions to work, and struggle in an easier and comfortable way in our Kurdish regions.

There is another equally important point we want to touch upon. In order for our people to be satisfied and aware of the course of things. Until the middle of the Syrian revolution, the terms of the Adana agreement were in effect between the Syrian and Turkish regimes, but after the Turkish position on the regime was clarified, the gap widened, and the differences between them, which reached to hostility, increased, and Syria also confirmed that the Turkish regime supported the armed groups in Idlib and Homs with arms and support, the terms of the Adana Agreement have been frozen on its own. The Syrian regime was hostile to our people and our movement, based on the requirements of the terms of the Adana agreement, and it was taking advantage from the Turkish regime, but after this agreement was frozen, it was no longer in favor of the Syrian regime to continue to implement terms unilaterally, without obtaining any gains from Turkey; So, in turn, it abandoned implement the terms of that agreement, and thus the regime retracted from its previous enmities in this period. On the other hand, the Turkish state agreed with the external opposition on the need to continue to implement the Adana Agreement, and to expand it in the event that they take over the reins of power in Syria. This is a prerequisite for the Turkish state in exchange for its support for the opposition, and we know that the opposition has acquiesced to this condition and accepted it. We believe that this matter is dangerous for us and our people in general.

- Everyone knows that the leader of the Democratic Union Party was chased in Syria, and he took refuge in the mountains, and stayed there for a long time, but he returned at the beginning of the Syrian revolution. There were many rumors circulating about an agreement between the head of the party and the Syrian regime, and that he had returned to the country at its request, especially since he was not arrested, and he was not subjected to any harassment after his return, and he is wandering around as he likes. Is there no truth in these rumors?

Party leader Abu Walat was in Iraq, and I personally met him there. I am fully aware of the details of his return to Syria, its circumstances, and I attended those discussions. The analyzes confirmed that the Syrian street has risen against the regime, and the Kurdish people have become an important and influential force in the country, and we have a strong and influential presence in the square.

And if Abu Walat returned to Syria the Syrian regime will not dare to arrest him because it will not be in its interest In these circumstances, and will not tolerate a direct war against the Kurdish people. But we want to say that this matter applies to all personalities and Kurdish politicians, and not only to Abu Walat. Abu Walat is not an ordinary person, but he is the head of a large Kurdish party, with a popular base that reaches 80 percent of the Kurdish street, and it is the most organized, and experienced party, and it would be foolish for the state to resort to winning the enmity of this huge popular mass. Our analyzes were like this, but on the other side there was no guarantee, so the return of Abu Walat was a great risk from him, and he expected all risks and possibilities, and it was a brave sacrifice from him and a step at the expense of his life. Despite all the risks, his return was necessary, and very important to advance the struggle, and unify the Kurdish ranks, and it was a historical and life necessity.

- Does this mean that he did not return at the request of the regime and with its help?

Neither the state nor the regime had any relation to his return, as his arrival was deemed a reality on the regime.

- So why it did not arrest him?

As we said that Mr. Abu Walat is not an ordinary person, and behind him there is a very strong force, however, if he was returning before the revolution, perhaps the state would have arrested or assassinated him, because the state's policy was that way at the time, and the regime had singled out the Kurdish people, and there was no voice or objection from the opposition, and external forces towards what happened in the Kurdish areas. At the time, the regime was taking advantage of anti-Kurds in its endeavors to get closer to Turkey, and through it to appease the West and America. But when Abu Walat returned, the scales had completely reversed. The powers, the states, the opposition, and the international and regional media, which were turning a blind eye to all the massacres, harassment, arrests, and crimes have happened in Syria and against the Kurdish people, have in turn, turned against the regime, which in turn has become aware that it will not be in its favor to win the enmity of the Kurdish people as well, and creating a stir not in its favor.

- The Syrian people have begun their revolution peacefully, but the regime has dealt with it, and it is still dealing with violence, the language of arms and repression. What is your position on the regime's suppression of the peaceful revolution and the uprising masses?

We are against the regime's resort to violence and weapons in suppressing the revolution; We condemn it, and we will never accept it. We do not and will not accept the killing of peaceful demonstrators under any pretext or reason. We say to the regime that your actions not only kill innocent people, but also accelerate your end, expand the rift that exists between you and society, prepare the ground for an endless civil war, and open the doors to external interference. The regime must immediately stop the repressive style, the language of arms and militarism in dealing with the peaceful Syrian revolution, otherwise the fate of the regime will be very bad.

The cycle of violence and internal strife will harm all Syrians, and will result in unimaginable consequences.

- Doesn't this regime draw lessons from the Iraqi and Libyan experience, and the rest of the other regimes that collapsed as a result of their intransigence and repressive methods towards their people?

The Syrian regime's structure appears to be ineligible, and is unwilling to undertake reforms and make the required changes; Because its organizational structure and mentality do not allow it to do so. For us, the issue is not of drawing lessons or not. What matters to us is the practical aspect on the ground. What we see on the ground proves to us that this regime did not draw lessons from the experiences that preceded it, and therefore we see its total dependence on the security and military solution, which will further aggravate the situation and slide the country into the gulf of great risks.

- Can we expect or wait for anything positive from this regime and take serious steps towards reform, democratic transformation, and guarantee liberties?

If violence and weapons do not stop in the country, real reforms are impossible, and it will not be possible to give us any hope. If this regime is true in his arguments about reform, he must first of all prepare the appropriate ground for this, and prove his seriousness; and that is through his immediate and total cessation of the language of arms, violence and repression. No reform can be successful in light of the existing violence, security and military discourse.

- Wouldn't the fate of the Syrian president be the same as that of the deposed presidents who preceded him, such as Hosni Mubarak, Zayn al-Abidin and Qadhafi? Is there another way for him to escape from this almost inevitable fate?

The situation in Syria is not the same as that of the countries you mentioned. There are differences between them, just as the international and external view toward these countries is not necessarily all the same, just as the situation of internal forces, especially the opposition, is not the same among the opposition forces of this country, and the social fabric of these countries is different to varying degrees. It would not be objective if we all likened it absolutely, just as it would not all go to the same point as this or that country. In the event that Bashar and his regime do not implement comprehensive and radical reforms in an immediate manner, his fate will not be similar to the fate of the other regimes. Rather, he will be much worse than their fate, and perhaps Syria will collapse and fragment completely.

- How do you see the Turkish role in Syria?

It is the worst and most dangerous role for the country. The biggest threat to Syria in general - and not just to the regime - is coming from Turkey. Turkey is manipulating Syria. Previously it sought to achieve its goals through the regime and the current president, and it succeeded to some extent in its goals, and it turned Syria into a state of its states, and used the regime in its dirty war against the Kurdish people. In the wake of the outbreak of the Syrian revolution, and Turkey became sure that this regime was inevitably departed, then Turkey turned to the opposition this time to continue its policy. Turkey supports the opposition, keeps it under its control, and its hegemony for the sake of weak Syria, under the rule, Turkish control, and a market attached to it. Erdogan looks at himself as if he is the president of Syria. Turkey wants to market the opposition on its soil to lead it to power in Syria; In order to complete its total control over the country, this is a very big danger for all Syrians, and not only for the Kurdish people.

- There are many politicians and political analyst who point out that the Turkish regime serves the Syrian regime a lot. By embracing parties of opposition on its soil. They say that this matter dispersed the opposition, divided its ranks, widened disputes and conflicts of interests among them, and thus weakened it, and this thing is in favor of the Syrian regime, according to their analyzes. What do you think of these analyzes? Does the Turkish regime serve the Syrian regime?

Yes, they are correct analyzes. Because Turkey imposes its agenda on the opposition, and insists that they come to it, walk according to its goals and plans, and work according to the program it draws for the opposition on its soil. It requires all parties of the opposition to hostility to the Kurdish people, and to deny their rights and national identity. And to stand against the Kurdish national struggle, not only in Syria, but in the whole region. It also requires them to accept the leadership of Turkey in the region. It requires the necessity for all to accept the domination of Islamic parties and political Islam to the reins of government in the country in the event that Assad goes away. There is a section of the opposition that has accepted these conditions of Turkey, because it needs Turkey's support for it, but another part of the opposition rejects this, just as large segments of the Syrian street do not accept the Turkish tutelage, and all of this has led to the division and dispersion of the opposition. Therefore, we can say that Turkey is the main responsible for the division of the Syrian opposition. We are confident that if Turkey did not interfere in Syrian affairs and opposition affairs, there would now be a real, strong and united national opposition in the Syrian arena, and such opposition could have expanded the revolution, strengthened it, pressured the regime, and reached all the desired goals of the revolution, without slipping into swamp of violence. But Turkey has offended the opposition, losing its legitimacy and cohesion.

- There are some parts and personalities that write and claim that you stand against the revolution in the Kurdish areas, that you threaten the Kurdish demonstrators, and prevent them from demonstrating against the regime, and that you are helping the regime to put down the revolution ... How true are these allegations?

If these allegations mean that we stand in the face of the application of Turkish plans in the Kurdish areas, and prevent from tampering with the Kurdish street, and turn the Kurds into soldiers to achieve the plans of the opposition that is in the Turkish bosom, if it means our deterrence of anybody that was shedding Kurdish blood to reach power, then we say: Yes, we will prevent any party and anybody from tampering with the Kurdish street, and we will stand against them. We have failed their goals and projects. We will not allow anyone to place the Kurdish people at the service of opposition parties' interests without having any national demands, without calling for their rights, and without raising their symbols, and without having any will or role in determining the goals that will be demonstrated for, under the names that the Kurdish people have nothing to do with. There are even parties that seek to move the Syrian and Kurdish streets with hidden fingers Like the helpless dolls, then we say: We will not allow this, yes, we did not and will not allow the Kurdish people to move under the banner of others, and under their slogans and demands.

As for those who claim that we did not allow the Kurdish people to participate in the Syrian revolution, these are false allegations, and they have no share of the truth, but our view is different from the view of those claiming to look at the revolution. Since the start of the Syrian revolution, and until now, we have demonstrated and have organized mass activities and events. Our people are the most people who have fought, revolted and demonstrated, and are still revolting for democracy, freedom, human rights and a decent life. Our fans and supporters have fought all these years, and they are still fighting for rights and rejecting injustice and repression. We attach great importance to the necessity of the participation of the Kurds in the Syrian popular revolution in our color, our privacy, and our voice, with the need to balance the general demands of the Syrian people and the Kurdish people. We are more involved in the Syrian revolution with our identity, colors and demands, and it is unfair to turn a blind eye to seeing that.

- Yes, there is action on the part of your movement, but we note that it is an extension of your struggle in Turkey and northern Kurdistan. Many are asking: Isn't it time for you to spend most of your attention towards the Syrian internal affairs and western Kurdistan, in order for this part to reach its freedom, and that it will not be sacrificed to the interests of the struggle in other parts?

Yes, there is a problem of this kind, especially a problem in finding a balance between the Kurdistan and Syrian dimensions. On the one hand, we have our jobs, and our responsibilities towards the Kurdistan issue in the rest of Kurdistan parts, and we also have basic tasks in each part separately, especially in western Kurdistan. Sometimes an imbalance occurs and there is no balance in this very sensitive equation. Sometimes we see that the Kurdistan dimension overshadows the internal dimension of this part, and sometimes we see the opposite. We seek to stop this imbalance, criticize the sources of error and weakness, as well as work to find more effective mechanisms in the struggle on the national dimension of Kurdistan and national levels in Syria.

This part has made great sacrifices, and served its national cause towards the rest of the parts with all its strength and determination, and was not hesitate with providing all that it required of it. Everyone owes this part. The payment of this debt will be possible if our efforts culminate in achieving freedom, and obtaining all national rights within this revolution.

We will work with all our energies to achieve this goal, whatever obstacles and difficulties we face. in order to ensure that the Kurdish people in western Kurdistan reach their freedom, we will provide all necessary support, we will make all the necessary sacrifices, and we will not hesitate with anything, and we will not evade from our national responsibilities towards western Kurdistan, as we are ready to provide all kinds of material and political support, Human, and military to protect the people and achieve their legitimate goals. We have taken the categorical decision of the necessity of liberating the Kurdish people in western Kurdistan as part of the popular revolution in the country, and we will not withdraw this decision completely. Therefore, our Kurdish masses must raise their own slogans, and demand national rights, in accordance with the peculiarities of western Kurdistan in the first place.

- You talked about the existence of a problem in the balance between the privacy of western Kurdistan, and other parts. Followers say that the flags, the pictures you raise, and the slogans that you proclaim in the streets of western Kurdistan are directed primarily to Turkey and northern Kurdistan, and the same is true for your discussions and speeches, and they ask, "Why do you direct attention towards Turkey? We have a Syrian regime that is not different from what in Turkey, and you turn the attention of the Kurdish people to northern Kurdistan, and it needs to rise and demonstrate for itself? " Doesn't this negatively affect your popularity in the Syrian street, and among the Kurdish masses in western Kurdistan?

We have our big masses, and our popularity is mainly known. The Kurdistan Freedom Movement entered this part from the start on the basis of the Kurdish dimension, and the people accepted it, wrapped around it, and adopted this approach. it did not hesitate on providing this movement with material, morale and human support. There are thousands of martyrs from this part, and there are thousands of them continuing to struggle at the highest levels in leading the revolution and the struggle in all parts. Seventy percent of the popular base is in this part supports this movement. However, the current circumstances make it imperative for the Kurdish people in western Kurdistan to participate in the Syrian revolution effectively, and with their identity and privacy, and they struggle to obtain their rights. Especially since the possibilities for victory and obtaining rights are available. The Kurdish people have struggled over these years to have amount of struggle, and a contribution to the revolution, and they are now picking the fruits of their struggle and their previous sacrifices.

Our greatest goal at the present time is to guarantee the freedom of the Kurdish people in western Kurdistan, and that they obtain all their rights. All activities must be organized in accordance with this objective. But at the same time we do not deny the emergence of some errors and deficiencies in the style, and the creation of effective working mechanisms, as errors sometimes occur in the practical form of the struggle, especially during marches and demonstrations. This is due to the old acquired habits that must be overcome at this stage.

The masses of our people enjoy a very strong patriotic and national feeling, especially since, part of their sons and daughters, struggle in other parts, and they are attacked by the Turkish and Iranian authorities, and some of them fall as martyrs for the sake of Kurdistan, and the national cause, and it is only natural that the people here express solidarity with their struggling sons and daughters, as well as the martyrs, and to express their anger, and to condemn the enemies and forces that kill their sons. But sometimes we notice it is gone too far for interest in the general Kurdistan issue at the expense of this part, and we are working to overcome This matter, and we seek to put all of our attention and direct all our energies and capabilities for the struggle in western Kurdistan, and that all our slogans be directed to the Syrian interior, and are directly related to western Kurdistan. Our marches, demonstrations and activities must be all aiming to achieve rights in western Kurdistan, and not anything else. We have developed a self-management project for western Kurdistan, and all our activities must be directed to the success of this project. We aim to make the national dimension in western Kurdistan the basis of our struggle at all levels.

- We hear a lot, and we read from some people, and those who say that they (they mean the movement) take the best of our children to sacrifice them in other parts. Also, some say that "these young people were seduced, deceived, and taken to wars they had nothing to do with, while they should have stayed here to fight for this part." And I ask: Are these young people so naive that they can be deceived? Indeed, wouldn't it have been better if they stayed here to fight in western Kurdistan?

This is an opinion, and a wrong view, many who say this with good intentions, and start from their ignorance of the facts, but there are some people and entities that broadcast such ideas knowingly. The Turkish state also says the same thing. It says, what are these (Syrians) doing here?" And it says that "all the leaders of the (guerilla) are from the Syrian Kurds, so what do they matter to us? Why do they come to war against us?" Even the Turkish state links the failure to solve the Kurdish issue in northern Kurdistan with leaders and leading cadres of Syrian origin. Here, too, there are parties that publish the same propaganda that does nothing to the Kurdish issue, as it is not subjective analyzes. Because above all we are Kurds, and we do not recognize the division that the enemies of our nation have made. Our homeland is Kurdistan and all parts of it are colonized, and there is no difference between this part or that. The Kurdish revolution, led by the Apogia movement, is a comprehensive patriotic national revolution, Kurds from all parts of Kurdistan struggle, in addition to displaced Kurds, and the number of militants from other nationalities such as Arabs, Turks, Germans, and Russians was not little among the ranks of the militants for the freedom of Kurdistan. These defensive forces are a national patriotic force defending the four parts of Kurdistan. Thirty percent of these forces consist of Kurds in eastern Kurdistan, there are thousands of militants and martyrs who joined from southern Kurdistan to the revolution, this thing is not confined only to the Kurds of western Kurdistan. Patriotism and nationalism are among the most important features of our revolutionary movement. We consider that the emergence of many senior leaders, and the leadership cadres from western Kurdistan, is a source of pride for this part. Today we see dozens of senior leaders and administrators in the movement from western Kurdistan. The people of western Kurdistan play their national and patriotic role towards the Kurdish nation in building institutions, leading the army, and resistance in All parts of Kurdistan and abroad. The other important point is that all these sacrifices did not go in vain, so if the Kurdish people in western Kurdistan were infused with the patriotic, nationalist and revolutionary spirit, then all that is due to the sacrifices they made within the Kurdish revolution, which created a revolutionary spirit and organizational awareness among the people. Also, the Kurdish fighters, who are fighting on the mountain peaks, are a source of courage to their families, relatives, and all patriots in western Kurdistan. I will say it frankly: If the regime on this day is approaching with all sensitivity from the Kurdish regions, and is working not to win the hostility of the Kurds, then this stems primarily from the presence of hundreds of sons and daughters of western Kurdistan within the Kurdish forces, and they are ready to defend their family and their part and protect it in the face of all attacks that might target them.

That is, there are thousands of guerrillas ready to sacrifice everything to protect and guarantee the freedom of this people. These guerilla cadres, who are fully dedicated to the Kurdish nation's service, are ready to return at any moment to defend their people here, to fight for their freedom, to build their institutions, to educate them, and to fail all the games that target them. The existence of such a large number of cadres is the basic guarantee for the freedom of the Kurdish people.

The same is true for the martyrs. Currently, there are three thousand martyrs from western Kurdistan, and they represent the honor, dignity and identity of western Kurdistan, they are the basis of our morale and national values, we will be loyal to them; Because they are the guarantee of the victory of our revolution, our attainment of freedom, and the attainment of all national and patriotic rights. In the near future we will give the name of all the martyrs to schools, streets, parks and national institutions, and this is the least we can do for them.

However, unfortunately, there are some Kurdish parties that imitate the enemies of our nation in their view of the martyrs, they do not consider them as martyrs of western Kurdistan; Because they were martyred outside it, and they say they are "martyrs of Turkey". We consider such hearsay and closeness as a great insult to us and our martyrs, and this is what we never accept.

We call on these people to retreat from these positions, and to correct their views.

- The Kurdish people in western Kurdistan contributed according to their energies in the revolutions of other parts, and made great sacrifices as you said, did not the time come for the other parts to return part of the favor of this part to them, and they start to support it in these sensitive circumstances?

I will not speak on behalf of other Kurdish nationalist movements, but I can say that the Kurdish revolutionary movement in general supports western Kurdistan, and it will increase its assistance more and more. The Kurdish revolutionary movement supports the struggle here financially, humanly and by media, and provides it with its struggle, political and organizational experiences.

We are benefiting from the previous experiences of the Kurdistan movement in building institutions and opening schools and service and social centers. The defense of this part, and the protection of its institutions, organizations, and all its social strata, is considered a debt in the necks of the Kurdish movement. Western Kurdistan has done a lot for the rest of the parts, and will therefore provide support and protection in times of need. But we have to rely on our strengths and our own capabilities in the first place, and we reach a level in which we can build our strength to defend our areas in western Kurdistan.

-What about southern Kurdistan?

We know that the Kurdistan Regional Government has its regional relations, legal obligations, and has its policies and official relations with neighboring countries, especially with Syria and Turkey, and perhaps these matters prevent them from public and direct support for the struggle in western Kurdistan, and its situation is very sensitive, and it has its internal problems, issues Pending with the central government.

- All Syrian cities raise the Syrian flag in marches and popular demonstrations, but you do not raise this flag, but rather raise your own flags. This matter has been the subject of many criticisms addressed at you. Is it

not better for you to raise the Syrian flag alone in your marches?

We are not against raising the Syrian flag, and we do not have any problem with it, just as we accept the Syrian identity as our national identity, we are Syrians, and we are an important part of the Syrian society, so if the Syrian people agree on this flag, and consider it a symbol of its symbols, we will also respect it, and we will raise it from time to time, but when they force us to raise the Syrian flag, and not to raise the Kurdish flags and symbols, this is another matter, and need a serious reading, as we raise the Syrian and Kurdish flags side by side. As a Kurd, we raise the Kurdish flags more and more intensively. But what we do not accept is considering the raising of the Kurdish flags is harmful and betrayal of the revolution. This is what we reject categorically. We see such positions as wrong and provocative, and we discern from them the external agenda; Especially the Turkish agenda and hands, and the Arab chauvinist opposition, so we are against such convergences, and we will not bow to any such provocations. We want to participate as Kurds in the Syrian popular revolution with our symbols, identity, colors, and peculiarities, and let the two flags fly. Syrian and Kurdish side by side, this will not weaken Syria, but rather will increase its strength and cohesion, and will ensure the success of the revolution.

- Some say that you do not only raise the Kurdish flags, but rather you raise many flags of the Kurdistan Worker's Party, and pictures of Mr. Abdullah Ocalan in your marches here. Why? You are not in Turkey, but in Syria and western Kurdistan?

We as a movement do not raise these flags in western Kurdistan, and we have no need for that, nor do we ask anyone to raise them. We are not asking anyone to raise the flags of the Workers' Party and (KCK) and other flags. It may not be raised, because not raising it will not be wrong, because Western Kurdistan has its peculiarities, features, parties, movement, and private institutions, as well as its expressions in particular. It would be best to raise (TEV-DEM) flags; But the popular masses bring their other flags, and raise them in marches, national events and demonstrations. But that does not reflect the movement's decisions for this part. As for the photos of Commander Ocalan, this is a completely different matter. The leader Ocalan is not only the leader of the Kurdish people in northern Kurdistan and Turkey, but he is a national leader, and a very large part of our Kurdish people in western Kurdistan consider him their leader, just as the leader Ocalan has fought for about twenty years in western Kurdistan, and he directly supervised the founding of The political organization and institution in western Kurdistan, Also, the majority of the Kurdish people in western Kurdistan adopt the ideology of Commander Ocalan, and it is very natural for them to raise his pictures and consider him a leader for them. Parties and other parts should respect this matter, and appreciate the will of the Kurdish people, especially since more than half a million adult Kurds signed several years ago (the leader Ocalan's political will represent me) in western Kurdistan.

We do not say anything to those who do not raise his pictures, but they must also respect the will of the people. Any party can raise pictures of Mulla Mustafa Barzani, or pictures of Mam Jalal, Kak Masoud, or any other Kurdish leader. We must respect the will of the masses as long as they do not antagonize the Kurdish national and patriotic cause.

- With regard to the Kurdish flag, some people ask: " From where did you bring this flag (yellow, red and green)? If you want to raise the Kurdish flag, then here is the known flag, so why you do not raise it?"

The flag "you call the flag of Kurdistan" is a modified version of the flag of the Mahabad Republic. It was accepted by the Kurdistan Regional Parliament, and it is raised in southern Kurdistan. Otherwise, there is no Kurdish national decision, or consensus to make this flag the national flag of all Kurds. Especially since the Kurdish people in the rest of the parts do not raise it except rarely. The Democratic Society Conference in Northern Kurdistan is the national parliament for Northern Kurdistan, and this parliament did not adopt this flag, but rather has its own flag, which is recognized by the people in the north. The same applies to the Kurds in the East, and we also did not officially adopt this flag and remains a flag for the Kurdistan region of Iraq, as well as there are Kurdish parties that raise this flag, everyone is free to raise this flag or not to raise it, and it cannot be imposed on anyone under any pretext. We, as the movement of the democratic society (TEVDEM), adopted the well-known Kurdish colors (green, red, and yellow) (kesk sor and zer), and we decided to raise this flag in western Kurdistan, and this is our natural right as a movement, but we do not impose this flag on any party whatsoever, and we also do not accept anyone to imposes another flag on us. But in the event that the Kurdish National Conference convenes, and all of them gather to raise a specific flag or draw a new flag, then we will also be quick to adopt it, and raise it along with the flags of our movement and our political organizations.

- The demonstrators in the Syrian street raise slogans such as: (the people want to topple the regime) , and (the people want to execute the president), and other slogans. But you do not raise these slogans, and there are also some other Kurdish and Syrian parties that do not echoing. so the Syrian street is divided into two parts; One section demands the overthrow of the regime, and another section does not want this. Do you still count on the survival of this regime? Do you not call the slogan of "toppling the regime" for this reason?

To date, no Kurdish party in western Kurdistan, nor the Kurdish movement in general in its aims have announced the overthrow of the regime; - If this is understood through the elimination of Bashar - no Kurdish party or organization has formally announced, and included in its publications, and in the words of its superiors about the demand (toppling the regime). That is, there is no division in the Kurdish movement on this issue. As for some of the youth coordination that are under the banner of the National Council in Turkey, it calls for (overthrowing the regime) publicly, and these coordinations represent only themselves, and do not represent the Kurdish street. Of course, there are some entities that practice duplication of positions, as they pretend to be with the slogan (toppling the regime), but they do not announce this within their official programs, because they seek to bid on the youth movement.

There is an entity named (the Syrian National Council) in Turkey, which comes out to us every week with new slogans, and it requires everyone to repeat those slogans without knowing them and what is the mechanism by which they choose these slogans and nomenclature, and they ask everyone to comply with them and walk under their command and their banner. However, as a Kurdish people, and as a revolutionary movement, we are not obligated to submit to the agenda of this council, and we will not compromise and turn into soldiers and serve them, in order to work for their goals and political aspirations. Especially since this council does not accept the Kurdish presence, does not recognize our rights, and considers the Kurdish revolutionary movement as a "terrorist". How can we accept such a council? How do we accept them? And to walk according to their will and raise slogans that emanate from them? Therefore, we did not agree to participate in the organized rallies under their influence and control. The dispute is not a matter of raising or not raising our slogans, but rather the topic is greater than that. We are a great revolutionary movement, and we have our weight in the region, a long history of militant struggle, countless sacrifices, and political experience that cannot be underestimated, as we have a million audience base, and we are not a few young people immersed in a political world and we will not acquiesce to any party that does not accept us and does not recognize us. We will not accept to acquiesce in them, and give up our will for their sake. They do not want to recognize us, they just want to use us, and turn us into a game with their own hands, and this is the main reason for the dispute, or to say our lack of agreement to protest with them.

Then do not forget that we have our own slogans, slogans calling for regime change, and for the national rights of the Kurdish people, and for freedom and democracy. And if the issue is confined to (overthrow), we have the slogan (toppling the repressive regime) and (ending the policy of denial in the Kurdish areas), and (ending the national smelting institutions), then we are stricter and radical than everyone in the matter of the fundamental change of the system, and its removal from the roots. We are not only against the regime, but against power of all kinds, against oppressive and dictatorial regimes of governance, and we call for power to be in the hands of society.

The important point that everyone should know is; We are not in the process of changing or overthrowing regimes in any country, and it is not only a matter of Syria. The Kurds have been fighting the Turkish state in northern Kurdistan for more than three decades, but they never sought, nor did they raise a slogan like; (Toppling the regime in Ankara) or (toppling Erdogan), and the same is true in Iran and Iraq. We have our own ideology, our own philosophical ideas, and base all our slogans on it.

- Your failure to raise the slogan (the people want to topple the regime) will not affect negatively your reputation among the Syrian people

Someone is using this to confuse us and distort our reputation among public opinion. There are also some Arab media organizations that previously pretended to be with us, and they were visiting us and claiming that they wanted to be our voice, because they were at odds with the Turkish state, so they were producing programs and films about us, visiting our sites, and broadcasting our news extensively.

But now it has turned to the side of Turkey, and it does not publish any news related to us that may disturb Turkey, so it does not allow us to present our view to Arab and Syrian public opinion.

- Some observers say that "your positions are vague to the public opinion, shrouded in uncertainty and ambiguity, and there is often confusion about your

positions, opinions, approaches to the opposition, power, Kurdish rights ... and so on." What is the reason for this ambiguity and this blurring?

There are some parties that seek to show our positions and our proposals as hazy and not explicit, and this is a method of psychological and media warfare directed against us. There are some entities that do not know the truth about our positions adequately, and we may be delinquent in expressing our positions, our goals and our projects more broadly in the media and in public opinion. I say it quite frankly; That we are neither with the external opposition nor with the regime. Rather, we represent strength, and the third alternative.

We believe that there are three main forces in the scene; The first force is the state and the regime, the second force is the external opposition represented by the National council in Turkey, and the third force is the democratic opposition represented by the National Coordination body for Democratic Change. We do not accept the division of the Syrian arena between two forces. The first is the state, and the second is the National Council only. This is not correct, and it is impossible for all the Syrian people to be, either with the state or with the external opposition only, but there are other alternatives and other forces, and we represent these Powers.

It is the parties that only want to link all opposition forces to the National Council, and put forth that our positions are blurry, because we are not with them. They accuse everyone who is not with them of being with the state, and this logic says: "Either you are with me or against me. "We consider that the coordination body represent us. Of course, this does not mean that the coordination body is the best model for the opposition, but its current program and its positions are more reasonable than those other two powers. We want the coordination body to be more powerful, effective and influential in the country's political life. We are not passive neutral, but we represent an important aspect of the revolution and the democratic opposition.

We are also against the regime and the authority, against all its repressive policies, and its approach to the Kurdish issue and public freedoms. We also confirm that we do not have any relations with this regime, and we are not ready to engage in dialogue or hold any relationship with it, nor are we with any dialogue with the regime in these circumstances, and within these conditions. At the same time, we are against the external opposition that denies the Kurdish existence, and does not recognize our national rights. Our positions are not completely blurry in this regard, we are against everyone who does not recognize us, and against everyone who practices violence, oppression and denial.

- Why is all this prejudice on your part from the external opposition? Are you against every opposition operating abroad? Do you consider external opposition always bad?

Not at all, we do not consider all parties of external opposition to be bad ... many of our comrades also struggle abroad, and we have held many conferences abroad, and we participated in many of them. But we are against the opposition, which relies on external forces, calls for foreign military intervention in the country, and counts on it to make a change in Syria. We are against the unprincipled opposition. What is wrong with this opposition that called the Kurdish people "terrorism" in an attempt to gain Turkish consent and support? We are against the opposition that approaches the logic of Machiavelli, and which sees all avenues permissible for it to reach its own goals, albeit at the expense of freedom and the cause of another people.

- But what is wrong with the opposition relying on the outside, especially on Turkey? This opposition also needs support. Then we do not forget that the Kurdish movement in northern Kurdistan has relied on the Syrian regime in its struggle against the Turkish state, so why do you begrudge the Syrian opposition to rely on Turkey?

We are the Kurds, and when the field was open to us to move in Syria, we did not stand against the Arab opposition, nor did we attribute it offensive nomenclature, nor did we question their eligibility, and the fairness of their case one day. We did not stand in the way of the opposition struggle, and we did not stand against the right of the Syrian people to freedom and liberty; Rather, we were part of a limited political agreement, and our war was primarily directed at Turkey. At the same time, history testifies that we did not fail to organize, educate, and train the Kurdish people on national and patriotic thought. We did not do what the external opposition is doing today, we never said: "let our affairs to pass, even if they are at the expense of the Kurdish people in western Kurdistan" and we did not ask the Kurdish people and the Syrian people not to organize themselves, or to demand their rights, and we did not say: "The Syrian democratic opposition is "terrorists. " But the Syrian opposition in Ankara does not do the same thing, but it is hostile to the Kurdish cause for its interests, as it signed the Adana Agreement that is hostile to the Kurdish people in Turkey and Syria, and called the struggle of the Kurdish people "terrorism. " Instead, of condemning the Turkish attacks on the Kurdistan region, and against the innocent Kurdish people, they are rushing to condemn the Kurdish revolutionary movement.

When Commander Ocalan was present in Syria, the friendship between the Kurdish people and the Arab people had reached the highest levels, and we had also developed very strong friendship with many Arab democratic and progressive organizations, and these organizations are today considered a very important part of the democratic and revolutionary movement in the country. In sum, we cannot compare the period of our presence abroad, and the presence of this council in Turkey at all.

- We all know that the Kurdish parties in other parts of Kurdistan have different relations with the Syrian regime. The Patriotic Union of Kurdistan had been established in Damascus, and Mam Jalal had good relations with the Syrian regime, and some time ago a message of solidarity was sent to this regime. Likewise, Kak Masoud has had strong friendship with the regime for decades. The same applies to the worker's Party, which had a good relationship with Syria before the signing of the Adana Agreement (1998). We know that these parties are influential internationally, regionally, and in Kurdistan. It is no secret to you that there is fear by many patriots in western Kurdistan, and they ask, "What is the guarantee that these (Kurdish) parties will not sacrifice western Kurdistan for their partisan and political interests?"

No party has sacrificed this part for the sake of its interests previously, nor we will be a victim of anyone now, nor in the future either. This is certain. The Patriotic Union of Kurdistan and the Kurdistan Democratic Party have their own official policy, and they are part of the State of Iraq, and they also have diplomatic relations with many countries, so Jalal is the president of Iraq, and represents Iraqi policy, and he cannot pursue a different policy from Iraqi general policy. Likewise, Kak Masoud is president of the Kurdistan region, practices politics, and has relations with all neighboring countries, including Syria. But this does not mean that they sacrifice western Kurdistan for their interests, this is out of the question.

We must put a general national and patriotic policy regarding western Kurdistan and Syria. This period requires such a unified national policy, and we, as a movement, see this as one of our primary functions. There should also be direct support for this part. However, the real and final guarantee for the victory of western Kurdistan, and its access to freedom, is primarily related to the people in western Kurdistan. Because the Kurdish national support for this part will be a catalyst, the main factor will be the extent of organization, strength and awareness of the people in western Kurdistan. This calls for the unification of the Kurdish political movement, and its non-association with the outside, so that it does not lose its independence, freedom of movement, and decision-making in a way that serves the Kurdish national cause.

- What do you link the lack of agreement of the Kurdish political movement on a unified political program and a comprehensive roadmap for the struggle to solve the Kurdish issue in western Kurdistan?

The main reason is that they are not independent. Every Kurdish party in western Kurdistan is in somehow linked to other parties. Some of them are related to the Kurdistan Region, especially the two major parties, YNK and PDK. There is a new part that has been linked to the National Council, the Brotherhood, and Turkey, and another part linked to the Syrian state. Therefore, it is difficult for them to be able to make their decisions independently and freely. Consequently, their unity is not possible under these conditions. Lack of independence leads, of course, to non-unity and agreement on a unified program and roadmap.

- The Kurdish parties met last spring within the initiative of the Kurdish National Movement parties, and issued a joint statement, but we did not see any repercussions for this initiative on the ground, and did

not result any serious developments on the path of unity at all levels. What do you relate that?

Unfortunately, it was a cosmetic unit, and it took place under the pressure of the Kurdish street. The revolution had just erupted in that period, and unity imposed itself on everyone, and neither side was able to evade the issue of unity, even if it was a formal unit. This process was at the initiative of the Democratic Union Party (PYD), so that the return of Abu Walat to western Kurdistan was for the sake of this unity. The initiative was a positive step in the beginning. However, we later saw that it remained a formality, superstructure, and was not reflected on the party base, or on the Kurdish street. The heads of the parties met every week and discussed all matters, then each party did what they liked without adhering to the decisions taken in these meetings. There were also rumors and counter-allegations by some parties against other parties on the street, especially against the PYD, and against its president and cadres.

As some of these parties were spreading rumors, accusations that the PYD came to sabotage Syria, and to sabotage western Kurdistan, and that it was an accomplice to the regime, these rumors were aimed at jamming, and defaming. There was a huge gap between words and deeds, between official opinion and behavior on the street. That is, the initiative did not develop into actual unity, and it remained formal, at the level of party leaders only. We believe that uniting political parties does not mean uniting the Kurdish people, because the parties represent only part of society and not society as a whole, and what concerns us is the unity of society, in addition to the unity of the Kurdish political movement.

- We see the dispersion and division of the Kurdish parties between the parties of the opposition. part of them is within the National Council in Turkey, another with the Damascus Declaration, also a part is with the National Coordination body, and one part is not involved in any parties of the opposition. What is the reason for this dispersion? Doesn't this fragmentation and division negatively affect the Kurdish issue and its strong representation in the national opposition?

Dispersion is not a positive thing, and it negatively affects the Kurdish street, and the masses confidence in the political movement. Therefore, we find that many independents are reluctant to participate, or not to participate in the political movement, as there is a large segment of the population that has not yet decided to contribute to the movement because of the fragmentation of the Kurdish political movement. It is true that the unification of the Kurdish parties does not automatically mean the unification of the Kurdish people, but the fragmentation of the Kurdish parties negatively affects the Kurdish people, and impedes the true unity of society. Moreover, this fragmentation opens the way for the opposition parts and external forces to easily pass their agenda to the Kurdish street.

The main reason, as we said in our previous answer; is the lack of independence. There is a very negative political culture in the political movement in western Kurdistan, which is that they do not trust their own strengths, do not believe in their energy and their own capabilities, and they are used to being associated with one side always. The Kurdish people outnumber the three million, and they are a very strong force, and they can transform into the strongest force in Syria in general, as their political, social and cultural movement has been united. they can be the main force, influencing and directing the rest of the Syrian movements.

But we see that there are anxiety and fear among some Kurdish parties that say: "We must improve our relations with the external opposition, so what will happen to us if it comes and receives power after the fall of this regime? We have to satisfy them in order to give us our rights." This psychological state is incorrect and wrong, and it must be eliminated directly, because it does not help us in anything. Knowing that we do not need anyone's consent, but the opposite is completely true, because everyone needs us, so if we all unite in one political program, all parties will rush to communicate with us, get us seriously, and solicit our support for them. Therefore, I repeat and repeat that we must get rid of the psychology of "inferiority and a feeling of weakness" and truly believe that we have great and very influential power, and that everyone needs to win the support of this force for them and not the opposite.

- What is the reason that prompted the Democratic Union Party to withdraw from the National Conference in western Kurdistan, although it was the most encouraging, and seeking to convene it, even it was the owner of the project and the initiative for such a

conference in the beginning, but it did not participate in it. What is the reason for that?

The Democratic Union Party did not withdraw from the conference, but was expelled and excluded. However, this exclusion did not take place directly and explicitly. We know that a decision was taken not to participate (PYD) at any cost in this conference, and the source of this decision was Ankara. Because they see PYD as part of the Worker's Party. However, this is not correct, as this party is the West Kurdistan party par excellence. The decision to remove the PYD from the conference was a decisive one; But this decision was applied in a very soft flexible manner. They demanded that the party participate as a number supplement, and without any influence, power or independent personality, otherwise they will not be allowed to participate, and this is what happened.

They know very well that it is impossible for the party to accept that it is merely a (number supplement) nor that it is impersonal and influencing such work. It is impossible for the party to accept to be as a tool for the sake of passing the policies of the National council and the Turks and accept the policies that it does not believe in.

The whole world knows that the Democratic Union Party has based its organization on the inheritance of the Kurdish revolutionary movement, and this movement has thousands of families of martyrs and families of militants, and it represents more than seventy percent of the popular base in this part. It is impossible for the party to accept these conditions, which are considered insulting to them. The participation of (PYD) in this conference, and under these conditions, does not strengthen the spirit of national unity but rather weaken it, because participation of this kind will make more than seventy percent of society in western Kurdistan politically paralyzed, and not represented in this conference. The mass base was dissatisfied with the PYD's participation in this way in such a conference. If PYD participated though, it would have lost his legitimacy with thousands of martyrs' families, militant families, national and youth institutions, women, and activity (PYD) submitted a proposal that independent members be elected by the people freely and democratically, but other parties did not accept the idea of independent members being elected by the people, but rather insisted on appointment by the parties, meaning that they would not be independent.

- What are the reasons that led other parties to refuse to elect the independent members?

Some parties have said that if independent members are elected by the people, PYD supporters will all succeed in reaching the conference as independents, and that the majority will be in their favor. They said it explicitly and directly to (PYD). However, they were publicly declaring that election conditions were not possible at this time. But we know that this argument is incorrect. We have held free and democratic elections for the Kurdish People's Assembly, in all Kurdish regions, and in Arab cities. This proved that elections are possible, and not impossible.

- The conference was held without the participation of the (PYD), many parties, political organizations, youth and other independent personalities, so where is the patriotism in this conference that excluded many?

This conference is not a national conference but rather a conference of parties, and it represents only the parties in it, in addition to some personalities. And it does not represent the Kurdish street, because more than seventy percent, of the Kurdish street are outside this conference, and will not accept any decisions issued by it. This means that any decisions made by it are not practicable on the ground. You also know that those in charge of this conference have relations with the (Syrian) National Council, and therefore they will turn this conference into a reserve power for the Syrian National Council in Turkey, with the aim of passing some of its decisions related to the Kurdish street. But we are sure that they will not succeed in that either,

because the Kurdish street is out of their control and influence. It is impossible for the Kurdish street to accept people (they claim to represent them) at this conference without having any role in choosing these actors. On the other side, there are some actors who have obtained tens of thousands of people vote to represent them in the People's Assembly, so which one will truly represent the Kurdish street?

- You talked about the issue of the Kurdish parties' connection with abroad, especially with the Kurdish parties in other parts. However, the Democratic Union Party (PYD) is said to be linked to the Kurdistan Worker Party. What is the nature of the relationship between the Kurdistan Movement and the Democratic Union Party?

The Democratic Union Party was founded in 2003 and was established as a private party for Western Kurdistan and Syria. All founders, leaders, and activists of this party are from western Kurdistan. In the year 2007, the Kurdish community system was established in western Kurdistan, and this system was the umbrella and the top roof for all struggling institutions, organizations and unions in western Kurdistan. Shortly before this year, the Democratic Society Movement (TEVDEM) was established. This movement adopts the ideas of Commander Ocalan. It is the primary and only relationship with the Kurdistan Worker's Party (PKK) and has no other organizational ties or relationships with the (PKK) nor any other Kurdish party. Relationships are intellectual and philosophical relationships only without going beyond organizational, political, and institutional relationships. Western Kurdistan has its own circumstances and its popular, political, cultural, and even independent geographic characteristics, so the PYD and PKK programs are different, and they cannot be the same.

- It is said that the Worker's Party does not allow the PYD to pursue politics according to the peculiarities of western Kurdistan independently. Some ask, "Isn't it time for the PYD to have the opportunity to be independent in its will and free to make its decisions in according to the realities of western Kurdistan without being instructed by Qandil?" Let (PYD) be an independent party, especially since you criticize the lack of independence of other Kurdish parties, as if you criticize something and come up with the same. What do you think of these pretentions issued by Kurdish activists?

I have to make it clear at the beginning that the PKK has changed a lot, and is not the same as it was before. It is no longer a classical Marxist-Leninist party, and it does not adopt party centrism, but rather has turned into an intellectual-philosophical party in the first place. it does not adopt the Communist style of parties, and the party is not considered a role model for society, but rather considers itself a pioneering intellectual party for the Kurdish revolutionary movement. That is, there is a big difference between the old (PKK) and the new (PKK). The PKK, re-established in 2005, represents a new model for democratic and pioneering parties. The PKK has no longer any organizational and special relations with Western Kurdistan, and its relations do not exceed the intellectual and philosophical side. The cadres of the political movement who are the sons and daughters of western Kurdistan who manage the struggle and organization in western Kurdistan independently and freely, and in a manner consistent with the national and patriot interests of the Kurdish people in this part in the first place. Like this criticisms go back to the past, especially before the years 2000 and 2005, because it is completely different now. Every cadre of militant cadres in western Kurdistan has very great experience, and accumulated struggle for more than twenty years, and they can manage the struggle on their own without the need for any external party. Many of these cadres have extensive experience in war, resistance, institution building, management of the organization, dealing with policy developments, and stage requirements; And they rose to the ranks of true leaders. Every leading cadre from western Kurdistan can return whenever he wants to western Kurdistan to continue the struggle in it. In the recent period, a very large number of these cadres and leaders returned, based on their personal proposal, to their country to respond to the sensitive stage this part is going through, and to ensure the protection of the people, and the attainment of their rights and freedom.

-Sometimes problems arise between your youth organizations and coordination in the street and during various demonstrations and activities. What is the cause of these problems and differences between you and youth coordination?

No, there are no contradictions between us and any of the youth coordination. They are the youth of our people, and they are enthusiastic, and contribute to this revolution, they have good intentions, a large part of them are supporters of our movement, and a large part of them are sons and daughters of our close families; (Families of martyrs, militants, and activists), and we are not against their contribution to the revolution and their positive activities. There are many coordination's close to us, which have weigh in the street on demonstrations and marches. The youth of our movement support them in many situations and circumstances, and participate in marches and demonstrations. We trust the youth, and we know they have revolutionary spirit and enthusiasm. We are only against those who try to pass foreign policies in the Kurdish areas, and to recruit masses for their favor. We are not against the slogan of (overthrowing the regime), we are also working on that with all the power we received, and this is not disputed, but we are against the raising of some slogans that they accept in principle. Like the "international protection" slogan, what does it mean to call for this slogan in the Kurdish regions? It means inviting the Turkish state to occupy western Kurdistan, because Turkey wants to intervene in Syria under the banner of (international protection), and under the pretext that the people want that. Sometimes Turkish flags are raised, and we are against that as well. We see that they are demonstrating under the slogan; (The Syrian-National Council represents me), No - by God - this council never represents the Kurdish people, and such slogans cannot be accepted in western Kurdistan. No one can protest in the name of the Kurdish people, and calls that the National Council (represents us), this council considers the Kurdish people (terrorists), calls on the Kurds not to ask their rights, denounces the Kurdish people defense of itself, and name the Kurds' defense of themselves with (terrorism), If this is the case then this council is also a terrorist. In conclusion, we say: We are not against youth coordination, we are with them, and we are ready to provide any assistance, as long as they do not serve external agendas.

- How true is your threat to them? And your hitting officials of some of these coordination?

We do not concede to do such actions, and we did not see any harm from them until we attacked them, and we do not need anything of this kind. They are enthusiastic youth, and they want to demonstrate and organize rallies, so let them do so, so what is the harm of that? We are a big movement, we have a lot of weight, and we don't concede to do these simple things. If we want to punish any person or party, we announce it without any fear or hesitation. But it seems that some of them do such acts, cast these accusations against us and stick such actions (which we are not satisfied with) to us. If we do not claim responsibility for anything, then this means that we have nothing to do with it. We are not afraid to tell the truth, and to announce everything we do.

-The age of the Kurdish political party movement has exceeded five decades in western Kurdistan, but - according to many opinions - "has not done much to the Kurdish people, and these parties, and these politicians and presidents, cannot respond to the request of the Kurdish street, and they are not open to change and renewal." , And suffer stagnation and hinder progress and openness. " According to your opinion, is it not time for the heads of the Kurdish parties to step aside to make way for young leaders and competencies?

It is not about old or new, everyone can play its appropriate role in political and militant life. Old politicians also have the right, especially those who have a long militant past, to contribute to any national movement today and tomorrow. No one has the right to impede others from the struggle because it is old or it is new. I do not see the correctness of such approaches to this topic. But we emphasize the following thing: If we are revolutionizing, and we call for change, to rebuild society, and to overthrow the regime, then we must be able to respond to the requirements of that, and to be real revolutionaries when we demand the revolution. And be free for this, and ready to sacrifice. As for the one who cannot sacrifice anything, is not ready to give any time for the sake of the revolution, and is not ready to relinquish any personal or family interest for the sake of the revolution and the struggle, he will not be able to lead the revolution or be a role model in this stage. Regardless of whether he is young or old, is he ready to sacrifice, devote himself and take responsibility or not? A young man who cannot be ready to break with the system, his institutions, his studies and his life form, such a young man will not be qualified to lead any real revolutionary movement, and hostile to the regime, can hardly be supportive and sympathetic to the revolution. Look at our cadres, they are completely cut off from the system, and they do not have any personal concerns or individual accounts, they are ready to sacrifice everything if required of them without hesitation or fear, because they are fighting and sacrificing for the sake of the Kurdish people, whoever wants to become a revolutionary and a leader must take the model of our cadres and militants role model for them.

- You always declare your stance against any external interference. Wouldn't the Syrian opposition have the right to demand external intervention, international protection to stop the bloodshed, and protect civilians from the regime's oppression and repression of the people?

Freedom and democracy cannot be expected and awaited through external interventions. Because states and external powers will intervene only for the sake of their interests before any other considerations. There is no need to deceive ourselves or to deceive others. It is impossible for America to come to bring to us freedom. The external forces have no concerns for freedom. Let us give the example of Bahrain. The Bahraini people demonstrated for freedom, democracy and justice, and an external intervention took place there, but this intervention was not aimed at helping the Bahraini people, but rather with the aim of suppressing its revolution, because its revolution is a threat to external interests. The same is seen in Yemen, where outside powers seek to help and support the regime and save it from the fall. However, at the same time, we saw the acceleration of countries and external forces to intervene in Libya with the aim of controlling the country's wealth and revenge on Muammar Gaddafi and his regime. However, we are not against activating international institutions, especially those that would prevent the Syrian regime from repressing the people, and provide supervision over the authority and protection of civilians. If such aid is activated, we will be at its side, and we will not object to it.

- The Syrian people started a peaceful revolution, but the regime initiated the killing, arrest, and torture of demonstrators, so what are the ways in which the Syrian people can protect themselves in the face of the arrogance regime?

Whatever the circumstances, developments, and provocations, the peaceful nature of the Syrian revolution must not be abandoned, because such regimes can only be overthrown by the massive mass uprisings, we must expand the scope of the popular revolution to the maximum extent that the regime will no longer be able to continue its repressive methods that will not benefit it. The Syrian people will guarantee their protection by strengthening the revolution, widening and amplifying it, and embracing it for all Syrians. The Egyptian revolution is the best proof of this, because the army retreated in front of the magnitude of the revolution, as well as the regime that made sure that killing the demonstrators would not help in putting down the revolution, because the numbers of demonstrators were increasing whenever one of them was killed by the regime. However, the Syrian revolution has not yet reached that totalitarianism, breadth, and magnitude. The Syrian revolution remained confined to some regions and governorates, as more than half of the Syrians are not involved in the revolution, and this weakens it, and makes the regime singled out to the regions one by one, and facilitates its control. If all the governorates make a single uprising, the regime will retreat and inevitably fall.

- We see that half of the Syrian governorates did not participate in the revolution as required, as governorates such as Aleppo, Al-Hasakah, Raqqa, As-Suwayda, Tartous, Lattakia and Quneitra, as well as the capital, Damascus, have not yet demonstrated. Why do you link the failure of these governorates to demonstrate against the regime?

There are many factors and causes. One of these reasons is that many social strata in these governorates have direct economic and interest relations with the regime, and the same applies to some clans and influential people in those governorates that do not see their interest in the departure of this regime. And another section does not participate, because it does not believe or trust the foreign opposition policy. To be more honest, they do not trust the Brotherhood, and they do not accept walking under the banner of the Brotherhood. There are some provinces, especially the southwest of which the Brotherhood is not accepted from the beginning, and the Brotherhood seems to have lost their influence in Aleppo as well.

- What about religious and national minorities such as the Armenians, Turkmen, Syriac, Druze and Circassians?

These minorities have not been reassured by the external opposition of the Brotherhood. Minorities are apprehensive, and they are unwilling to contribute to something that they do not see their future in, and that does not guarantee their interests and rights. This does not mean that they are with the regime, but the opposition program has not yet reassured them. The Alevis, Druze, Christians and Kurds do not see their interests and guarantee their rights in this opposition. If the opposition had a more democratic and receptive program for diversity, and the mosaic present in the country, the participation of minorities would be stronger and more effective than it is now.

- Do you have relations with these minorities?

In the past, we had specific relations with some of the personalities of these minorities, but our relations developed more within the stage of the popular revolution, and they turned into institutional and organizational relations, friendship, alliance, and solidarity aimed at solidarity and support in this sensitive stage our country is going through. We hope to take some practical steps on the ground to increase rapprochement and coordination among us in a way that serves all our interests.

- We see fear by Christians in particular at this stage. What is the cause of all this fear? What scares them?

They are right to fear from the opposition under the Brotherhood's wing. Because the Brotherhood advocates the need for the Sunni majority to dominate political life in the country, and this matter raises the concerns of all classes, especially Christian minorities. If the majority of Christians are either with the regime, or stand on the neutral, it is because they are not satisfied with the opposition's proposals, especially the Muslim Brotherhood. They consider the theses of this opposition more backward than the theses of the current regime regarding them.

-What is the future of Kurdish-Arab relations in Syria?

The relationship will be based on free citizenship. The Arabs are well aware that the Kurdish people have an important position and strategic role in changing the balance of power, and that without alliance with the Kurds, none of their attempts to perpetuate and reach the desired strategic goals can succeed. Everyone has become aware that it is impossible for the Syrian national unity to be established with pressure, killing, intimidation, denial and exclusion. Moreover, the opposition forces have realized that it is not possible to succeed in the democratic revolution and reach building a free democratic system without the Kurds' participation and recognition as a basic component in the country.

Freedom cannot be achieved without the Kurds. Recent events have confirmed the weight and size of the Kurdish people, its organizational strength and its political role that cannot be overlooked or denied. The Arab brothers realized this well, and they are now seeking to establish good relations with the Kurdish people on this basis. Also, the Kurdish people have become aware of their true strength and distinctive role in the Syrian arena. We believe that the Kurdish and Arab relations are moving towards their true historical character on the basis of friendship.

- Will the Kurdish people reach their rights and guarantee their freedom in the end within this revolution? Will the Kurdish people win? What are the guarantees?

Of course, there are some dangers that stare the national gains of the Kurdish people, especially in the event of the Kurds practicing any wrong policies. If the Kurds did not participate effectively and with their own identity in this revolution, and put their national and patriotic rights in the second degree or neglected them under the pretext (it is not the time of Kurdish rights), and if the Kurds did not participate by their free will and content themselves to be tools in the hands of others, then the Kurdish people will not benefit with something of this revolution, they will leave it empty-handed, but will lose everything that they obtained during the long years of struggle and work. For all that, caution is very important, because history is ruthless, and so will future generations curse us a thousand times, because we have not taken advantage of this historic opportunity that is not repeated much.

The Kurdish people should not postpone the claim of their rights, they must remain demanding their rights at all levels, on all occasions, and not stop placing their demands and rights before the authority, opposition, and world powers. And to strive to obtain firm guarantees in exchange for any work, participation, or any alliance they submit. Personally, I am very optimistic, because there are responsible and real policies pursued by the Kurdish movement, and the Kurdish people are closely watching all of this, and they do not accept any imbalance or negligence. Also, as a movement, we have not only decided to formulate policies, but have also started to take practical steps in this period in an accelerated manner and, especially in building political, cultural, social and educational institutions, and we will continue to do so in order to guarantee the full rights of our people.

- There are some cases of killings of demonstrators in Syrian cities, and some opposition figures have turned toward the language of weapons ... Can we talk about the danger of a civil war staring in Syria that we may live in the future?

Yes, there is a risk of civil war in the country, and it is a very high possibility. If violence continues, this will lead to civil war. In the event of an external military intervention, civil war will inevitably break out. Syria is not like Libya, nor is it like other countries, because it has many minorities and components, and these minorities will not accept solutions imposed on them by force of arms, and will fight strongly.

- In the event of a civil war break out, who will be the warring parties?

Everyone will slide into this swamp. The Alevis and Sunnis will fight to the end. Likewise, the Kurdish people will resort to defending themselves against all attacks that may target their existence, rights and gains. The Kurdish people will not stand by any of the warring parties, but it may be subjected to a Turkish attack, and the attack of the Arab chauvinists against the Kurds is a possible matter. That is, all forces and components will slip into internal warfare with or without their will, and Syria will turn into open fronts for hostility and internal fighting. As a result, Syria will be the main loser in all of this.

- Are the Kurdish forces in the rest of the parts ready to defend the people in western Kurdistan in the event of a civil war, or if they are exposed to any attack or aggression?

Any Kurdish Kurdistan national power is charged with defending all the Kurdish people in the four parts. Consequently, it is not a force specific to a specific part of Kurdistan. It is mandated and responsible for defending the Kurdish people in Western Kurdistan as well, if necessary. Any national force defending and protecting the Kurdish people in western Kurdistan is considered a sacred duty of that force. However, I repeat that it is our duty to self-organize and organize our youth in western Kurdistan within a protection organization that will defend our regions, cities, villages, and lanes in distant cities. We have to rely on our own strengths, accelerate the organization of youth well and be cautious of any negative developments that may happen in the country.

We made the decision to defend western Kurdistan under all circumstances, and we will do whatever is required of us in this regard without delay, and we will do our job properly. Let everyone be reassured in this regard.

- There are rumors in the Kurdish and Syrian streets that a number of (Guerilla) forces have moved to Syria recently?

No, nothing of this kind has happened, and there is no need for that at this time. However, everything required was done to ensure the protection and defense of western Kurdistan. We want everyone to be reassured that we have done everything necessary during the past seven months, and we have taken the necessary measures to form an organizational mechanism for young people from western Kurdistan for protection and self-defense. We seek to deliver this mechanism to the highest levels of efficiency and readiness to protect and defend western Kurdistan and prevent any aggression that our region may be exposed to. But if we see that this mechanism is not enough, then we will not hesitate to seek help from our brothers when needed.

- It is noted that the fierce war and battles between the Kurdish Guerilla forces and the Turkish army, as well as the Iranian army, are intensifying. Commenting on this, some people wrote: "The Kurdish Guerillas are fighting by proxy for the Syrian regime in order to

reduce pressure on it and distract the Turkish state with this war so that it cannot increase its pressure on the Syrian regime." How true are these sayings and analyzes? Is it reasonable that Guerilla increases its attacks on Turkey and Iran as fulfillment reciprocate to the Syrian regime?

Any fulfillment?! Which reciprocate?! This regime, ten years ago, is fighting us, suppressing us, and burning green and dry in our regions. This regime has handed over more than one hundred and fifty cadres of the Kurdish movement to the Turkish authorities and assassinated and killed dozens of our leaders. it did not leave a supporter, sympathetic, and active for us and arrested, tortured, and insulted them all. Which reciprocate are they talking about? Rather, the Syrian regime must hurry to compensate the Kurdish people, apologize, and ask for forgiveness for what it committed against us. We do not have any debts or obligations towards the Syrian state and the Baathist regime. This state must change its policies towards the Kurdish people, correct its mistakes, and compensate the people for all the tragedies and grievances that it was subjected to by this unjust regime.

As for these rumors, and the false propaganda that targets us is issued by one center, we know this center well, and we have a long time with it. This center is nothing but the special war circle of the Turkish state, and they have a local network here in Syria as well, the mission of this network is to spread and broadcast such rumors among the popular masses, and on the Internet. It is very unfortunate that some Kurds also transmit such rumors knowingly or ignorantly, but as a result they contribute to propaganda, rumors that hostile to the Kurdistan revolutionary movement, and its national struggle.

Recently, a lot of this local network was exposed. The National council revealed its condition and showed its true face, especially when it sent a telegram to the Turkish authorities, denouncing the resistance of the Kurdish revolutionary movement and its legitimate struggle, and calling it (terrorism).

We say the exact opposite. There were secret negotiations between the Kurdish revolutionary movement in northern Kurdistan and the Turkish state, and these negotiations had reached a very advanced level. They continued to speak with Commander Ocalan at Imrali Prison until it came to signing the protocols.

There were also official discussions and negotiations between the leaders of the Kurdish movement and the Turkish state in the Norwegian capital, Oslo, and it was just around the corner to reach the final result. In order to make way for the development of these negotiations and their success, the Kurdish movement took the initiative to extend the freezing of its military operations for a year and a half. But once the popular revolution began in Syria, and the field became open for the Kurds to organize, and the struggle in western Kurdistan and Syria in general, and to form a mechanism to defend our masses here, and ensure that it obtained its full national and patriotic rights. The Turkish state was afraid of this matter, so initially rushed to the forces in the Kurdistan region of Iraq, and asked them to agree against us, and to work together in Syria and western Kurdistan, but it didn't get it there. It was precisely in that period when the war broke out between the guerilla and the Iranian army. We cannot separate the outbreak of this war from the events in Syria. The Iranian state launched this war in order to hinder the Kurds from focusing on Syria and directing their attention to it, with the aim of alleviating the Syrian regime. The same applies to the Turkish state, which struck negotiations, violated the armistice without warning, and intensified its attacks against the Guerilla forces, the Kurdish people in the north, and the regions of southern Kurdistan, and on democratic institutions as it imposed severe isolation on the leader Ocalan in an unprecedented way. And all of this in order to prevent the Kurds from focusing on Syria. It also continues its brutal attacks, using all internationally prohibited weapons, and in violation of all rules of war and human values, and has assassinated many leaders. in front of all this, it is only natural that the Kurdish revolutionary movement will defend itself and respond to intense attacks against it. But the owners of these rumors turn things upside down. The Turkish state launched this war against the Kurdish movement, in order not to be able to work for the benefit of the Kurdish people in western Kurdistan. not the opposite.

- let us suppose that the Syrian popular revolution was aborted, and the regime succeeded in suppressing it. Then will the regime not return to its former era, suppress the Kurdish people and return to its old methods? Is not the Kurdish people exposed to such a risk in the event of the failure of the Syrian revolution?

We do not believe that the regime - if it does not fall - will return to its previous era. Change is inevitable in Syria in the event of the departure of this regime or its survival, because the matter is not related to the people and those in power, but rather is an inevitable. That is, this regime will change if it leaves or remains in power, as the people no longer accept this life, and these unjust methods. Also, emerging regional conditions and international powers will never accept this regime in the present form. The only chance for this regime to survive is entirely linked to radical changes and real democratic reforms, and above all its policies towards the Kurdish people. It is impossible for this regime to remain if it does not change its approaches to the Kurdish issue through a fundamental change. Also, the path of reforms passes through changing the current policy towards the Kurdish people, and ending the chauvinist policy towards the Kurdish areas.

- You always express your rejection and warning about the issue of bloodshed in the Kurdish areas. It seems that you are "too sensitive" as some say, and there are those who say: "You are the last to be entitled to fear bloodshed, because every day you offer many martyrs

and blood in the mountains." How do we read your warnings? As well as these rumors issued by some Kurds?

We believe that blood should not be shed unless it is within the framework of legitimate defense. Also, we do not sanctify violence, neither here, nor anywhere else, nor do we see violence as a means of change, nor do we use violence to reach strategic goals, nor for regime change. We use violence and weapons within the framework of legitimate defense. That is, we defend ourselves in the event of attacks against us, whatever their source. However, the situation is completely different in western Kurdistan. Currently, there are no direct military attacks against the Kurdish people. Except for some arrests of some activists and for short periods, there are no attacks, and there are no obstacles to the Kurdish people organizing their ranks, building their institutions, and peaceful and democratic expression of their demands.

Also, the regime does not target the youth who rise on Fridays, and they demand the overthrow of the regime and the execution of the president. So Is there a need to give our blood without any cause or benefit?

I will be more candid with you, as we are ready to sacrifice our souls, give our blood for the freedom of our people, for our rights, and to defend our national gains in all parts, but we are not ready to waste one drop of any Kurdish blood in order to bring down any regime, not in Ankara, Neither in Tehran, nor Baghdad or Damascus. We will not waste our blood to change rulers, and bring in other rulers. But at the same time, we are ready to sacrifice our lives a thousand times for the rights of our people, and to guarantee their freedom in all of Kurdistan, especially in western Kurdistan. In the event that our people are attacked here, we will not dawdle to sacrifice ourselves to defend it, and deter all attacks, even if this requires us to provide five thousand martyrs, we will not hesitate to do so.

We will not allow shedding the Kurdish blood, and only because the blood is shed in Daraa and Homs. We will not allow the Kurdish blood to be wasted, because someone is sitting in Istanbul, pushing us to death, and striving to turn the Kurdish region into a battleground for war and death. And everyone who seeks to shed the Kurdish blood for the interests of others, he is a traitor, and we will be against them. Kurdish blood is never cheap.

-It is said that the vast majority of your mass base are poor and illiterate, and that they are not educated. So why do intellectuals turn away from you and not contribute to your activities? As if there is a gap between you and the educated people, where is the error?

This is not true ... We know that the majority of our base are from the poor, workers and villagers, and this is a matter of pride for us, and there is nothing wrong with that, because we are a movement of the poor and the oppressed in the first place. Also, we are not an organization for the elite, but a popular and mass organization. We have a wide mass between students, and educated people. Unfortunately, however, it seems that hostile politics and media war have particularly affected the educated segment more than others.

We consider it a positive thing because the educated segment does not accept everything directly, and it prefers accountability, and trial always, and this is positive, and we never stand against that. But there are some who are affected by the malicious campaigns against us by some parties, especially on Internet pages.

Nevertheless, our popular base among the educated and conscious segment of doctors, lawyers, professors, artists, and writers is never a few.

- It is said that you "do not accept the criticisms directed against you, that you threaten those who criticize you, and that you even eliminate them physically?" Why you do not accept criticism, and do you really eliminate those who criticize you, or disagree with you?

In recent years we have undertaken the largest self-criticism and revision campaign in the past few years. We have made a comprehensive criticize for all the struggle's level, form, and working style, as well as renewing and changing our concept and organizational structure. That is, we are in a stage of criticism and self-criticism. But it seems that we have a problem defining the Kurdish street with the changes and reforms that we have made to many of our working methods, goals, and organizational relationships. We need constant review, and criticism, in order to be able to keep pace with the times, to respond to the requirements of the stage, to represent the street fully, and to meet the aspirations of the Kurdish people.

We are not against criticism, nor do we have any wrong approaches to critics. Our hearts are wide, and accommodate all constructive criticisms that criticize our ideas, our working methods, and the form of our struggle. But sometimes it happens that some unjust charges and attacks provoke some of our cadres and supporters. Frequently, some criticisms deviate from objectivity, and reach the level of insulting, and attacking values and sanctities, and this cannot be called (criticism). We are militants, and revolutionaries sacrifice everything for freedom and the rights of the Kurdish nation, but some come out and say the worst words about us. like regime supporter (Shabeeha of al-Nezam) and (state agents), then these sayings cannot be considered as (criticism), but rather they attack, betray, insult, and despise, and many friends and supporters do not accept this, and express their reaction to that, and this is their natural right It is unfair to accuse activists and cadres who sacrifice their lives and souls for the sake of the homeland unfairly, and by slandering with traitors and agents. So what if the accuser of these accusations are people who live their daily lives with all the comfort or employees in the institutions of this regime, receive their salary from the state, study in the schools and universities of the regime, and serve in the regime's army, meaning that it is linked in a thousand form and form to the institutions of the regime; How can they accuse people completely cut off from personal life and cut off from the regime as agents, shabeeha and traitors?

- Whenever we open a newspaper, magazine or any website, we will find something related to you. You are always on the agenda, and the subject of media discussions and its interactions, whether positive or negative, why you are always the main concern of the media and rumors?

The reason is that we are constantly moving, working, and renewed. Before the outbreak of the Syrian revolution, we had been relatively out of the media agenda, especially since we had retreated to a certain degree from the political scene and the limelight due to the increasing pressure from the authorities on us, and the number of our cadres had decreased a lot because many of them were arrested. But after the recent events, we made a very big leap, and many of our cadres returned to the country, and vitality and activity returned to our mass base, and we launched many organizational, popular, and militant campaigns, as we presented many special practical projects, and we took many steps. All of this was reflected directly on the street, and the media sometimes positively, and negative sometimes. If this indicates something, it indicates that we are working intensively. We also act boldly, and take bold and new steps, and all new and unfamiliar steps arouse admiration for some and are irritating for others.

THE THIRD CHAPTER

The Political Project

- In one sentence, what do you want to achieve for western Kurdistan as a final project?

We want for western Kurdistan the self-administration, because it is the most reasonable and correct solution for the people of Western Kurdistan.

- How can you summarize a general definition of self-administration, what is it?

Self-administration is far from the concept of power, and it is linked to society, and not like classic self-administration. It means that society in western Kurdistan manages itself in all political, social and economic aspect by building its cultural, economic and political institutions. Through these institutions, a political decision is made, and it establishes the following: a legal will whose function is to solve social problems, and a cultural will to solve cultural issues ... etc., in short; In order for society to solve all its problems by itself, and for that purpose it establishes its institutions, and develops. In self-administration, society builds its administration in all aspects, so that it develops naturally without facing obstacles hindering it.

- You were talking about the Democratic Confederation and the Democratic Republic, where did these projects go? What is the relationship of self-administration with it? Why did the names of your projects change?

Our projects have not completely changed in essence, we have developed our new philosophy since 2000, and crystallized in its final form in 2005. We introduced the Democratic Confederation, and therefore self-administration is the essence of the Democratic Confederation, and it is a form of democratic confederation.

- It is said: "You follow northern Kurdistan in your policies. When they talk about a project, you are talking about it here, when they talked about the democratic society system, and you also put it up for western Kurdistan, and when they put forward the project of self-administration, you also put it up for

western Kurdistan. " Do you imitate northern Kurdistan? Why is that?

No, here it is not related to Northern Kurdistan; But we, as a movement, possess a project and see it suitable for all Kurds, all societies, and it is suitable for Arabs, Kurds, Persians and Turks together, all the peoples of the Middle East. We see it as the right form as a project, and everyone can apply it according to its circumstances. It cannot be applied in all places in the same way, as northern Kurdistan differs from its west and from other places. There are many differences, for example: The revolution in northern Kurdistan is an armed revolution, and the people live there under the weight of the ongoing war; As for here in Syria, the people are in a state of peaceful popular revolution, and so far they have not turned to arms. The struggle here is a political struggle, and therefore self-management will be different.

- And why do you not demand a confederation, autonomy or even secession?

This is our philosophy we are far from all forms of power, as we reject all projects linked to the state. For example, it is impossible for us to demand a state, so how do we demand a state, while we are fighting state thought and power?! Federalism comes in the same sense of authority, and so does autonomy. Our philosophy is against all kinds and forms of power. The solution we seek to implement is totally linked to society. We do not want authority in place of authority, nor a state substitute for a state, but rather we want a democratic society. If there is authority, then it will be the authority of society. The society wants to run itself in all aspect without there being any obstacles or super authority. Society deserves direct democracy. In short: The project that we want is not the democracy of the state, nor the democracy of power, but rather the direct democracy of a society that guarantees all its rights, and guarantees its freedom and its natural development. It is not important to be in power, or not to be. Rather, the most important thing is that we are the basis, and with the passage of time, power will weaken and disappear.

- Is there no opportunity to implement federalism? What prevents the Kurds from obtaining a federation similar to their brothers in southern Kurdistan?

We can start the struggle in western Kurdistan for federalism, and we get it, but that will not be the final solution for solving the issues of people and society in western Kurdistan, and it has geographical, political, and social reasons. We reject it from the principle of rejecting power; We do not think in terms of the pragmatic aspect that saying: "If we have a very strong force, we have called for federalism and autonomy, or the independent state of Kurdistan." We reject authority in all its forms, and this is our philosophy. Federalism needs the people to be fully prepared, and that the Arabs will accept that as well, but the Arabs have not yet recognized our existence, our language, and our culture. Likewise, the Kurdish people must be prepared to make very big sacrifices. But in the end, federalism is not the ideal form for a society to live democratically and freely. We are confident that the Democratic Confederation, in its practical form, which is represented by self-administration in western Kurdistan, will provide the Kurdish people with their rights, obtain their freedom more, will live in a more democracy, and be independent.

- But do not forget that there is an existing state in which you live, and a regime that controls this state and has its constitution, laws and power ... Will this state allow you to build your self-administration with ease?

Now in western Kurdistan, there is a great opportunity to achieve self-management, which in essence comes in a sense; The more the state shrinks, the more society democracy will emerge. Whenever society owns institutions and departments, it will be able to weaken the state. Society builds a system of self-administration at the expense of the weakness of the state, so that the state will not exist and society will develop. These conditions are now available in western Kurdistan. This people fought a lot, made sacrifices and martyrs, and organized itself, and today it has had an opportunity to build its own administration. Today, state institutions in the Kurdish regions have become meaningless in all military, economic and political aspects, and a great vacuum has occurred here. It is the right of the Kurdish people to build their institutions, organize themselves, and build their administration to fill the void, and this is a natural right for the Kurds. With the start of the Syrian revolution, we saw the appropriate circumstance to start the process of building self-administration. We have noticed community acceptance of these practical steps on the path to building management institutions. The power of the state is weakening, and we can impose our presence on the state and develop society. In this way, no matter how the authorities and regime change, society will maintain its organization without any influence, and its presence will be imposed on everyone.

- What is the meaning of the political will of society? How will this will be established? How will it look and how it works?

Yes, it is an important question, and its answer will be very important. The political will of society is organized from the bottom up, that is, it establishes the bodies that make decisions from the population centers; From the bottom to the top of the base pyramid. No one will be appointed from outside (without the will of society) to represent and decide on behalf of it, and there will not be an external body that works to represent society, as is the case in representative democracy, that is, state democracy. As for the democracy of society, it becomes a priority for self-administration, whereby each community must make decisions regarding its direct affairs. This mechanism starts from villages, neighborhoods, cities and districts, regions, and even reaches every square in western Kurdistan. In order to ensure this, each village must have its own political council, and the village's political decision will be taken from there, consciously, and the members of those councils can present their ideas, The same applies to every region that must have its expanded council so that decisions are taken in a more comprehensive manner, and at the same time they have active participation in the political decision-making process in the provinces. The same applies to the provinces, where there should be bodies representing the provinces such as Afrin, Kobani, Qamishlo, Derek ... etc. The district council is very expanded, and political decisions are made for the community in the district. The Supreme Council is the general coordinator of these councils. The Supreme Council does not take decisions for the councils, but rather coordinates between the councils to take joint decisions, especially those related to public affairs that exceed the affairs of a single district. Thus, a political reference will be established from the bottom up.

- You recently started the elections for the People's Assembly for Western Kurdistan, what is the function of this assembly? s it an alternative to the Kurdish conference or is it a private Kurdish parliament? What will its job be, and what is the goal of its foundation?

True, this council is like the parliament of the Kurdish people, which will be a reference for discussing, proposing and resolving all issues and problems of society at all levels and aspects, and not only from the political side. This council will play the role of the Legislative Council. That is, this assembly not only represents us, but rather represents the entire Kurdish people in western Kurdistan, especially since the majority of society has participated in the election of this assembly. It represents the will and vote of tens of thousands of people who participated in the elections.

- Before the announcement of founding the Democratic Society Movement (TEV DEM), (KCK

Rojava) the Democratic society system was in place, and had its flag, constitution, organization and institutions. So you dissolve that system, and you announced the democratic society movement? what's the difference between them? And why did you do that? Was this just a name change?

KCK Rojava (Democratic Society System) was established before the revolution in Syria, and the situation was different then, and there were fierce pressures and attacks against us, in those circumstances we announced this system almost secretly, compulsively, and in difficult circumstances, in a narrow framework and its institutions were limited and secret. The members of those institutions were subject to arrest and permanent prosecution, and therefore the organizational structure was limited and confined to a very narrow framework, but with the start of the revolution where different circumstances were born, and there was a greater margin of freedom. In order to open the way for everyone to join the organization in a more flexible manner, Major goals include everyone, for everyone to participate in the process of building self-administration, where it was necessary to establish a comprehensive movement with a broader framework, in which case it is normal for the name to change as well. For example: At KCK we were appointing people to do jobs as a result of state pressure now it is done through elections.

- The political side dominates you, and you link everything to politics? In this dialogue we often talk about society and its role. As if you just discovered the community. What are the social aspects of your political movement?

The dominant aspects of our movement are social aspects, and basically our movement is a social movement. Originally; There is no society separate from politics, and it is impossible to separate the social aspect from the politician. Our main goal is to build a democratic society. The political aspect is considered a part of social activity and a dimension of it. Yes, the political aspect was the dominate of our movement at the beginning of its emergence in western Kurdistan, and Kurdistan dimension was dominating on other aspects, so political awareness came first of all, with the aim of educating society, especially since the people were ignorant of what was going on around it from Policies and plans, as his national and Kurdistan consciousness was weak, so political awareness was necessary above all. And there had to be a real revolution within society, which we can call a revolution of emission. It was a political revolution in its content. As a result, there are people who are sacrificed, a people aware of themselves.

Now is the time to build on that foundation an ethical and political society. Community serve and developing social aspects will be a top priority for us. The establishment of each union or institution will be based on community service. Building and establishing everything will be to serve the community. The establishment of organizations and unions must not come on the basis of the ideological aspect as we previously wanted it, but should be for the sake of serving the community, and therefore any union, institution or organization must be formed on this basis.

The difference between the democratic society movement and our old organization lies precisely on this point. Also, it should not be union on a political basis, but on a social, service basis. Even those who will join the democratic society movement, it is not a condition that they support our movement, and it is not a condition that they adopt our philosophy, that of the leader Apo, but they must serve the society and work for it, and they are not required to leave their political organizations or resign from them. Accordingly, we can say: Regulation is the organization of democratic self-administration, it is the organization of the people and society, and its political aspects do not concern us, and we must open the door for everyone to serve his society and his people.

- After we published the special handbook (Practical Projects for Building self-administration) , which you referred to planning to build hospitals, clinics, and organizing the private health sector. Then many people - surprised - wondered about the possibility of this?

Right, we talked about that earlier in that brochure, and now I'm going to explain that further; The health problem is a basic problem in society, and there are two parties who can do this; One of them is the state's powers, meaning that it is under the domination of the state, and the other party is the commercial private sector, and it was confirmed that society is being exploited by both parties. For example, in Syria, the public sector is run according to the interests of the regime and influential persons, and it is marred by a lot of favoritism, bribery, and corruption. The private sector also cannot response to all segments of society, because the poor cannot go to private hospitals and therefore cannot receive the necessary treatment. Since we say: We will build a democratic society, we must solve the health problem as well; This requires a healthy system away from the corrupt state system and the greed of the private sector. This will be possible by establishing communes, and this is the third and right alternative. Therefore, all those involved in the health sector, including doctors, nurses, paramedics and technicians, will be organized in order to serve the community for free, in addition to continuing their private work. They will be employed to educate the community in terms of health. The first step for making that project work is regulation. For example, the regulating doctor will treat a number of people every month for free, and the same applies to the pharmacist, who will give each month a free amount of medicine for patients. Soon we will have the ability to establish and organize this without relying on state institutions; Initially, we will form health centers in the Kurdish areas, and over time, hospitals will be built. We discussed this idea with health professionals, and they, in turn, understood this service project for society, and many of them became voluntary and enthusiastic. They have started building clinics, and this is the first step, and all this is done with the support of the people.

- There are social diseases and pests prevalent among some segments of society in western Kurdistan, such as drug use, drink, smuggling and poverty. What are your mechanisms to treat such pests?

There are two mechanisms we follow in the self-administration project; The first mechanism is awareness, which is the basis, by organizing awareness committees specializing in these matters within the communes and local councils. Since some cannot be persuaded by educational committees, there is another mechanism, and this mechanism is the Commune Commission for Discipline, which is charged with tackling corruption, social scourges and combating corrupt people. Also, there are popular committees, which are semi-secret, whose mission is to preserve society in all aspects, to combat danger and social diseases, and to compel deterrents who harm society. Of course, the popular committees will not interfere unless the methods of awareness and discipline fail with them. There is the drug problem that has wasted the youth and harmed society, as well as the morally widespread problems resulting from poverty, displacement, and special war policies hostile to the Kurdish people. For all of this we need a large awareness campaign to address these problems, and there must also be practical steps by pressure from the popular committees.

- On the cultural side, you recently opened cultural centers and established bands. Have your cultural projects stopped there? Or are there other projects?

These were only the first steps, and they emerged as a result of the interim need for them, and it was necessary to take these steps; Like the opening of Kurdish language schools, art and culture centers, it is still in its development stage. We have taken the decision to open Kurdish schools in all Kurdish regions, and perhaps the number of schools reaches thousands, the Kurdish Language Foundation is charged with carrying out this campaign. The same applies to the centers of culture and art, which must exist in all Kurdish regions and cities, and no one will be able to stand in front of the aspirations and requirements of society. These steps will be constantly evolving, and we will not be satisfied with what exists. Culturally, there will be awareness centers for women and youth, and kindergartens will be opened for children in their mother tongue. A large organization for undergraduate students will be established. We will work to build all the institutions and cultural centers that serve the community, in order for this society to be aware of its culture. We are still in the beginning of the first step.

-Some say that you open these centers and schools with the permission of the regime? Did you obtain a license from the state?

No, there is no license, and these centers were opened as de facto. And if you want the truth, it has been opened to fill the existing vacuum, depending on the strength and capabilities of the people. The opening of these centers was thoroughly discussed and studied among us, and on that basis we opened these centers. The authorities of the regime expressed their concern and dissatisfaction with that, and they threaten us as well, but the authority has not been able to do anything as long as there is strength and organization of the people. A while ago, in a village, the regime forces raided the village in order to close the Kurdish Language Center, but the people rose up against those forces and rallied around the center and did not allow them to raid or close it, and after tension, the regime forces acquiesced to the people and returned unsuccessfully without result. The regime at this time oscillates between staying and falling, and it understands the sensitivity of its position and calculates a thousand time for everything in this region, and therefore it is not ready to confront the Kurdish people for the sake of these schools and cultural centers, the regime at this stage will not fight the Kurds because they learn their language and develop their arts and culture; So he accepted this thing as a fait accompli. We will not leave this opportunity and we will continue our struggle.

- What is the future of these schools? Will it be official and recognized by the government in the coming days?

A great struggle and hard work is required in order to gain the formal character of these schools and centers and to give them an appropriate formula in the Syrian constitution. We are confident that when our institutions and centers play their role effectively and substantially, they must impose themselves on this regime or others; This regime or the regime that will replace it must accept this thing as a fait accompli. But as long as they refuse to do so, we must fight and fight against them. Perhaps we have not yet fought a great deal to change the regime in Damascus, but we are ready to provide anything to protect our centers and institutions, and we will struggle greatly to ensure that our institutions get formalized in the constitution.

- You open centers, institutions, and establish many projects. Where do you get the money to finance these projects?

The source of financing is, without a doubt, the people. The people give everything to finance the opening of their centers, they serve themselves day by day, and provide assistance within their capabilities. But when we plan to undertake large projects, we resort to collecting donations among the people, and by that we provide financing for these projects. At this time, we are carrying out a large fundraising campaign, it is a large and comprehensive campaign, and our campaign is still ongoing until now, quarter of this campaign will be devoted to the measures that we take to protect the region in the face of wars and possible attacks, especially in order to provide the requirements of the special popular committees. We have dedicated a portion of these donations to open institutions. Of course, the people did not fail in this regard. There are also many rich and well-off from our supporters, and they, on their part, have given us a lot, providing homes and sites to be schools, centers and institutions. We did not seek help from any other party, and only we were dependent on the people.

- On the occasion of your talk about the rich and well-off from the Kurds in western Kurdistan, is there a role for the bourgeois class, the rich and the Kurdish merchants at this stage?

There are no very rich people in western Kurdistan, so the word "bourgeois" is not really meaningful in western Kurdistan. There are people with capital, from merchants, landowners, investors, and others. Some of them provide the assistance needed to open centers, institutions, and to support the revolution. The situation is different now, we build a social system, and we build institutions for society, and this is a project that concerns the whole society, and not for a specific group, and not for the sake of a specific political thought; So everyone contributes to provide support without exception. Until the pre-revolutionary period, material support for the movement was restricted to supporters only. But now we have passed that stage, where we are building projects for everyone without exception, away from politics and intellectual inclinations, but only for the service of society. This requires the wealthy to provide all support for the sake of it, and this will be fair and acceptable to society, but if they do not provide the support and assistance required of them, there will be a class disparity in society, and it will not be fair, as the poor donate and the rich refrain.

- You talked about the People's Committees? What are these committees What are their jobs? are they a substitute for the police? And the security forces? Or are they secret military forces?

These are civilian forces, not military ones, and we can say that these committees are disciplinary committees. A great vacuum has occurred here, when the regime withdrew from some places and cities, so we must fill this vacuum to maintain the organization and discipline of society, and to protect it from chaos and disregard for its security, so the People Protection Committees must be established. There have been many recent robberies, and large quantities of narcotic drugs and contraband were smuggled into the region for the purpose of disseminating them within society, and chaos and moral and ethical issues occurred, so the formation of the People's Committees for Protection was aimed at controlling the region's security. These committees take its order from local councils in the villages, neighborhoods, or regions. They are organized committees whose primary goal is to protect society, maintain order and discipline. We will work to develop and expand its field and increase its numbers, according to the conditions that may arise in the region.

- There are cases of intentional killing of Kurdish soldiers in the army, and Kurdish families are concerned about the lives of their children, especially

those recruited in the revolted areas. Isn't it time to encourage Kurdish youth to split from the army? And return to their areas? And if they split, is there a specific mechanism to absorb them and organize them within society? Or benefit from them in the formation of Kurdish forces?

Of course, it is very good that the Kurdish soldiers not slide into any civil war, and stay away from these dangers and conflicts. Our position is clear on this that the Kurdish youth must not serve in the regime's army and forces, and this position is not new. Our position is not the result of current circumstances, but rather our position long ago. We do not serve the regime and the state that controls, and exploits society. Kurdish youth should go towards the Kurdish revolution, and volunteer to fight enemies. Young Kurds in the four parts of Kurdistan, instead of joining the armies of the occupied countries of Kurdistan, and standing in the ranks of an army fighting their people, they must join the ranks of the Kurdish revolution, and fight for their people, and protect their community, and their homeland. The correct place for Kurdish youth is to be in the ranks of the Kurdish Revolutionary Forces. The right place for

Kurdish youth is to join this revolution, not to stand against the people. We are living a historic opportunity and we should take advantage of it and not to miss it.

- On some issues, you have touched on the media and the press. We notice a whirlwind and storms from the media ... the media has become a force cannot be underestimated. There are the media of the regime, of the opposition, and the external media, and each media outlet has its goals, tools and methods in creating the event and directing the masses. But we, the Kurds, do not have a strong media. Do you have projects to establish a strong and alternative media that can influence and create the event?

There are two-way media; Where there is a regime media, known for its lies, its denial of facts, and it moves according to the dictates of the regime and its interests, and there is no place for the Kurds in it. And there is the external media that enabled to prove its worthy in the recent period, as they did not have a strong presence before. Arab Gulf channels (such as Al-Jazeera, Al-Arabiya, and others) move according to their interests, and the Kurds have no place in this media either. All the media are totally blind to everything that happens to the Kurds, and everything that the Kurds do is not reflected in them, as if the Kurds are not present. And these media broadcast, amplify and promote everything that is in its interest and serve its policies. Much of the truth remains hidden. When it comes to the Kurds, and their rights they turn a blind eye on everything, or distort the truth or turn the facts. The existing media does not represent the reality of western Kurdistan. Likewise, the existing Kurdish media, most of which are related to parties. Partisan media does not serve all groups of society, so we need a comprehensive media that is inclusive of all. The establishment of strong Kurdish media does not require the fall of the regime in order to proceed ... In this vacuum, we can rely on self-administration to establish a large and influential media institution, we need a television channel that can be the voice of western Kurdistan, and a news agency that can transmit the news in its moment, and to Media network to be the mouthpiece of the Kurdish people. We need a comprehensive media organization that represents society in its various directions and inclinations. Time is a time to show all our social, cultural, political and reality in a professional and creative way to all of the world. Capabilities are available, and we've started with some steps.

- The regime recently granted Syrian nationalities and identities to Kurds deprived of all their civil rights, who had been stripped of them in the past, especially in the Al-Jazeera region. How do you evaluate this step?

This is a misnomer. It should have been a restoration of nationality, not grants. But in the end it is a good move, not a bad one. But we do not need the (Arab) nationality, we are Kurds. We say: It is a good step from the humanitarian point of view, as those who obtain it can exercise some of their human rights. But we, as Kurds, must enjoy our own national identity in the new Syria.

- In the recent period, the "Parties Law" was issued by the regime. How serious is this law?

This is linked to the future of Syria. When there is a democratic dialogue, a democratic constitution, and a democratic change, and the parties are able to operate freely and freely announce their programs and ideas, only then this law will be serious. However, the issuance of the "parties law" without a serious change in the constitution makes no sense. We will await the new constitution, and we will act accordingly then.

- What are the points that you demand for inclusion in the "new constitution", especially regarding the rights and status of the Kurdish people?

The Kurdish demand for the new constitution is: the democratic self-administration. On this basis, the Kurdish people can manage themselves in all regions and at all levels.

- Among the new laws, the "Media Law" was issued by the regime, so did you benefit from that? Is there a possibility to practice free media in Syria?

The main problem; There are no practical steps, but words more than action. But as a result, if there is an opportunity, we will benefit from it, but until this moment, there are no serious practical steps. Wherever we find an opportunity, we will benefit from it. For example, in northern Kurdistan, thousands of militants were martyred until there was a free media space, meaning that it did not happen on its own. We are ready to make any efforts or sacrifices to obtain freedom of the media in western Kurdistan. In this revolution, the opportunity was created to create a free outlet for the media.

- You said in your speech that "the Syrian regime does not want to confront the Kurdish street, nor to get close to it," but in return there are many of your supporters and cadres in the regime's prisons, what do you link to that?

The first reason is the regime and Turkey; In other words, relations have not been broken until now, and the Syrian regime is still pinning hopes on the Turkish state. The other reason; It is that the regime has not explicitly announced its position on the Kurds. As for its current position on the Kurdish street, it is a tactical position and it has no clear position. The regime is against the organization of the Kurds and their unity. As for our comrades who were released, they ended their sentence, then they were released, and the amnesty did not include them.

- Some say that "when you do demonstrations, the regime does not come close to you, but when others demonstrate, they are attacked by the regime and its Shabeeha (groups of supporters)." What are the backgrounds of this case?

We are also being arrested, and many of our supporters have been arrested during demonstrations, and they have not been released yet. Of course, there are some Kurds who have contacts with the outside, and the state faces them badly. It is a mistake for the Kurds to deal with some external part. it is better for the Kurds to struggle, sacrifice, and be arrested for their rights, and for their struggle, and not for the implementation of orders from some external parties. The majority of those arrested recently were not arrested because they were Kurds, but rather because they considered themselves part of the external opposition, and they act accordingly.

- A short time ago, the Kurdish politician Meshaal Tamu was killed. Why Meshaal Tammo? And why in Qamishlo specifically?

This was a serious plot targeting the Kurds. We didn't find the truth about who killed him, but the aim of his killing was to spread chaos on the Kurdish street, waste Kurdish blood, and push the Kurdish street to react. Some forces did a lot to incite the Kurdish street and made it random. These forces tried to use the killing of Meshaal Tammo to push the Kurdish people to serve the external opposition, and to open a new front in Qamishlo city. The largest beneficiary is the Turkish state. But those forces did not succeed in that, and their plot failed. And the Kurdish street did not slip into these games and acted with rationality and caution.

Thank you very much for your generosity and for your answers to these questions.

October 27, 2011

Derek-Rojava

Printed in Great Britain
by Amazon